SUVLA BAY AND THE RIDGE FROM TURKISH SAP ON LALA BABA

G. DRUMMOND FISH
R.N. RIFLES.

IMBROS
(Sir Ian Hamilton's Headquarters)

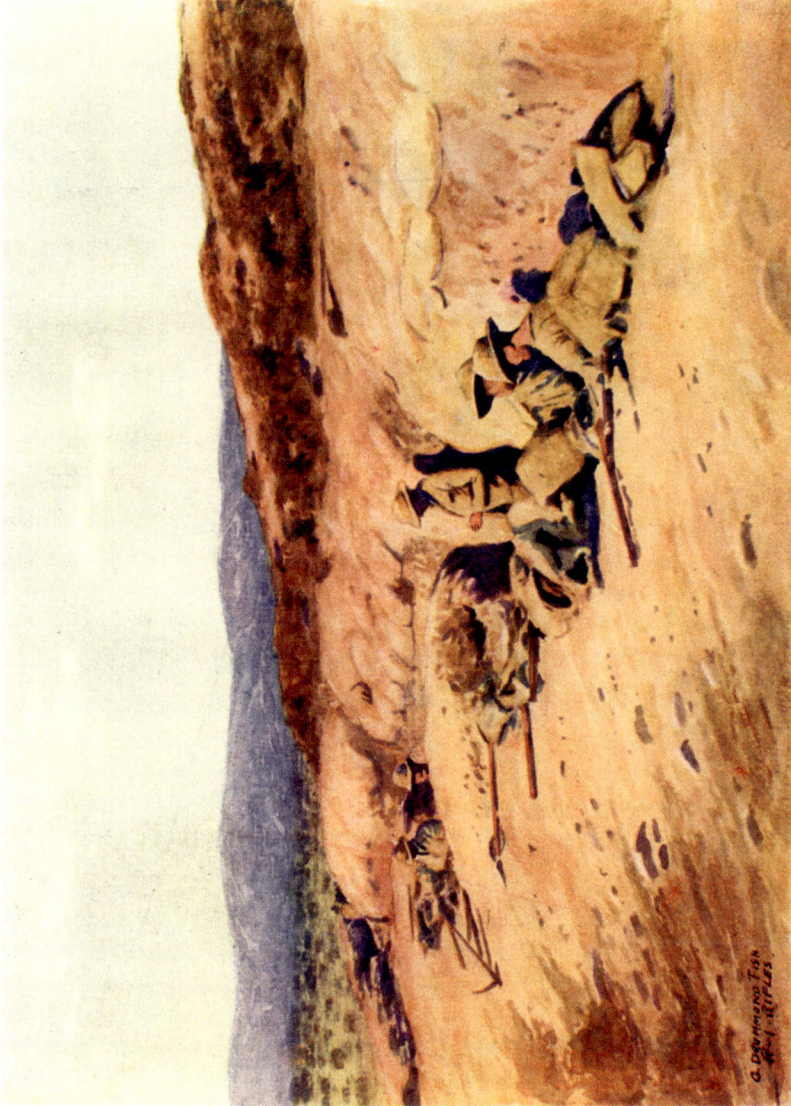

G. DRUMMOND FISH
R.I. RIFLES

"D" COMPANY, 7th R.D.F., IN TRENCHES AT CHOCOLATE HILL
(*From a Photograph*)

SUVLA BAY FROM SUVLA POINT
(*From a Photograph*)

SALT LAKE, CHOCOLATE HILL, AND ISMAIL OGLU TEPE

"C" BEACH AND ANAFARTA PLAIN; CHOCOLATE HILL IN THE DISTANCE

SHIPPING, WOUNDED BY NIGHT

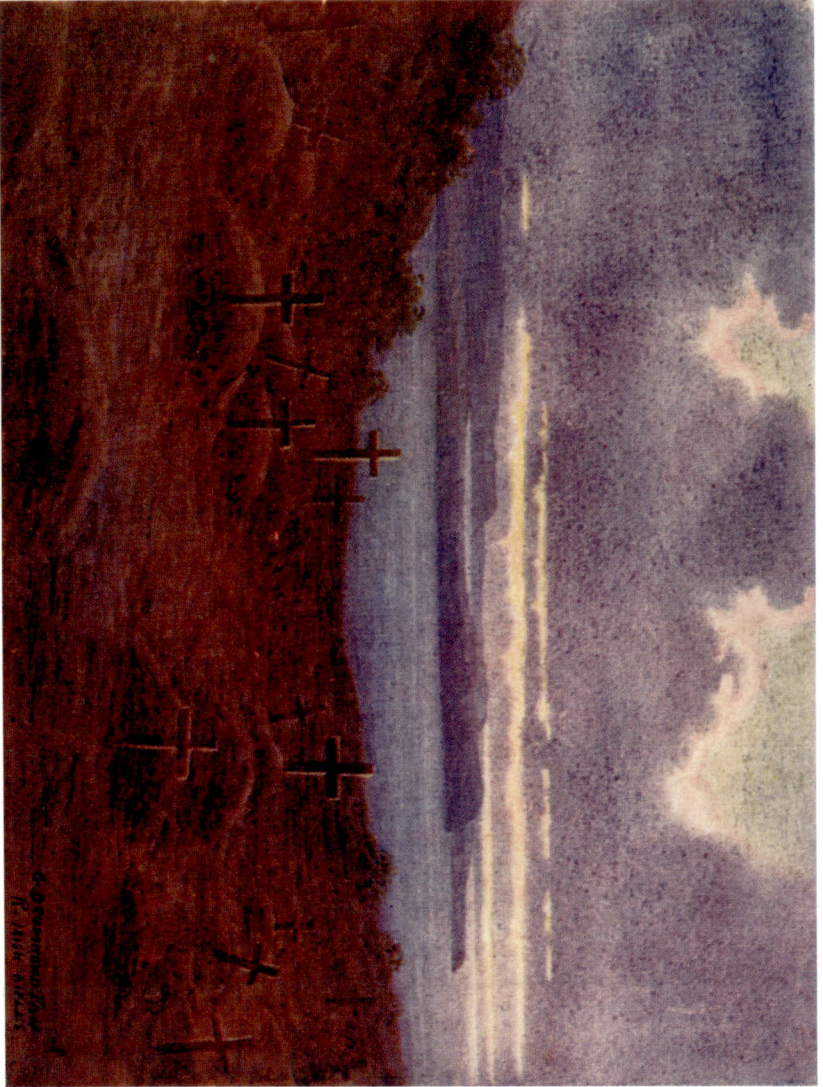

HALLOWED GROUND AT SUVLA BAY

THE PALS AT
SUVLA BAY

THE PALS AT SUVLA BAY

BEING THE RECORD OF "D" COMPANY
OF THE 7TH ROYAL DUBLIN FUSILIERS

BY HENRY HANNA, K.C.

WITH A FOREWORD BY

LIEUT.-GENERAL SIR BRYAN T. MAHON
C.B., K.C.V.O., D.S.O.

PUBLISHED BY
E. PONSONBY LTD., 116 GRAFTON STREET
DUBLIN

PRINTED AND BOUND BY ANTONY ROWE LTD
EASTBOURNE

PREFACE

WHEN the war-cloud burst over Europe in August 1914 and the call came from Lord Kitchener for a hundred thousand men, there were none answered more readily or realized more keenly their duty as citizens than those who were afterwards known as the Dublin " Pals." Content to join and fight together as privates in one regiment, the 7th Royal Dublin Fusiliers, they have helped by their valour to add another thrilling page to the history of the Irish regiments in the Great War. Though Ireland shall long mourn the loss of those who found their last resting-places on the hill-sides of Suvla Bay, she shall ever remember with pride, no less their splendid patriotism than their heroic deeds and stubborn resistance against the Turks.

This is a record of the rank and file. It has been written as a memorial to our brave dead of " D " Company of the 7th Royal Dublin Fusiliers. We owed it to them that this should be done. Though it deals primarily with the " Pals," it is because the material was more readily procurable. It has been a real regret that I had not the material for the other equally gallant companies of the battalion, nor for their sister battalion, the 6th Royal Dublin Fusiliers, who bore the burden of much heavy fighting under their distinguished leader Colonel Cox.

The book has been prepared under the auspices and with the helpful advice of a committee of well-known Dublin gentlemen whose names appear in the Appendix. Willing help has been given where asked. The survivors and relatives

PREFACE

of the members of " D " Company have been most kind in allowing letters and diaries to be perused and in lending photographs to be reproduced. Lieutenant Drummond Fish has permitted the reproduction in the book of his beautiful water-colour sketches, which give such a vivid portrayal of the actual scenes in which the military operations were conducted. He went through the campaign until wounded, and by reason of his official duties in sketching for military purposes he was able to observe and note correctly the natural features and colours of the country.

Mr. Harold G. Leask, President of the Architectural Association of Ireland, has drawn the excellent maps of the Peninsula, Sulva Bay, and the Kizlar Dagh Range.

Mr. H. A. V. Spencer, Army Instructor, has skilfully prepared the interesting contour sections, which will convey to the lay mind the natural obstacles and difficulties to be surmounted by the troops.

Ponsonby Ltd., the well-known Dublin publishers and booksellers, have with great public spirit given their services gratuitously in the publication and distribution of the book, and I should like to mention specially the assistance in technical matters so kindly given me by Mr. Cyril Ponsonby while preparing for press.

As for myself, it has been a labour of love.

HENRY HANNA

54 LANSDOWNE ROAD, DUBLIN
October 1916

6

FOREWORD

BY

LIEUTENANT-GENERAL SIR BRYAN T. MAHON, C.B., K.C.V.O., D.S.O.

COMMANDING THE TENTH (IRISH) DIVISION

I HAVE been asked to write a " Foreword " for this book about the " Pals " of the 7th (Service) Battalion of the Royal Dublin Fusiliers. It is a pleasure for me to do so, as no more gallant battalion ever left the shores of Ireland. They were well trained and disciplined, with a high and patriotic sense of duty.

They covered themselves with glory on the 7th of August 1915, in their advance and subsequent successful attack with the bayonet on Chocolate and Green Hills, and on many other occasions, not only on the Peninsula, but later in Serbia. For these deeds their name will ever stand high in the annals of the British Army.

There was one company (" D ") composed almost entirely of Dublin gentlemen, and the City of Dublin may well be proud of this gallant and heroic band. In my opinion it was unexcelled in the British Army for bravery, dash, discipline, and a sense of duty. They lost very heavily at Suvla, and I asked those that remained to volunteer as officers, who were then urgently needed. Though it was a wrench to break up their company and leave their comrades, their sense of duty made them go where their services were most required. I cannot give them higher praise than to say that as officers they served as well as they did when privates.

In conclusion, I would like to place on record the help my gallant friend, Mr. F. H. Browning, gave in raising this battalion. In his efforts he spared no trouble and obtained more recruits, both officers and men, than any one in Ireland. This brave gentleman was killed during the late rising in Dublin, when in command of a company of his Volunteers. It was a sad fate for one who had done so much for Dublin, both by helping to raise the 7th Royal Dublin Fusiliers and also in leading the Dublin sportsmen so often to victory for many years at cricket and football.

The 7th Battalion of the Royal Dublin Fusiliers was up to strength a few weeks after Lord Kitchener gave the order to raise the Tenth Division. Would that the splendid example of these men were followed by the Irishmen of to-day!

B. MAHON
LT.-GENERAL

October 21, 1916

CONTENTS

ILLUSTRATIONS

IN COLOUR

11

THE HAPPY WARRIORS

CLEAR came the call; they leapt to arms and died
As in old days the heroes prayed to do;
Great though our sorrow, greater yet our pride,
    O Gallant Hearts, in you.

Surely they sleep content, our valiant dead,
Fallen untimely in the savage strife;
They have but followed whither duty led,
    To find a fuller life.

Who then are we to grudge the bitter price
Of this our land inviolate through the years,
Or mar the splendour of their sacrifice
    That is too high for tears?

Ours be the Spartan joy, the Spartan pride,
In those who were our comrades in old days;
To such, whose names for ever shall abide,
    Give we, not tears, but praise.

For them no more the stirring bugles call,
Their labours over and their battles done;
But, lo! on us the instant duties fall—
    Our task is but begun.

A. L. F.

CHAPTER I

THE PALS

WITHIN a week or ten days of the outbreak of the war, F. H. Browning, the President of the Irish Rugby Football Union for 1914, issued a circular to the Rugby Football Clubs in the Dublin district calling upon them to urge their members to place their services at the disposal of the country in carrying through the war which had just begun. As soon as he discovered that there would be a large and ready response, he inaugurated the Volunteer Corps, subsequently known as the Irish Rugby Football Union Volunteer Corps, having its headquarters at the well-known Lansdowne Road Football Grounds, Dublin.

As Mr. Browning subsequently died from wounds received by him at Northumberland Road, Dublin, during the Sinn Fein Rebellion of Easter week, 1916, while returning with his Volunteers to Beggarsbush Barracks, we may record here the tribute paid to him in the epitaph upon his tombstone, erected to his memory by the members of the Irish Rugby Football Union Volunteer Corps : " He will live in the memory of all as an honourable comrade and true and distinguished sportsman, who by his untiring efforts and splendid patriotism obtained from his Corps over three hundred recruits for His Majesty's Forces during the Great European War."

He perceived at once that the Corps could be made a nucleus for recruiting, while working on the basis of a volunteer force for home defence, and he extended its membership to men not only from football but all other athletic clubs. He engaged several drill sergeants, and inside a few weeks had hundreds of business and professional men from the City, both young and old, learning the elements of military instruction and drill. It was a sight quite as unusual as it was thrilling to see these men, after their day's work in the City, parading in platoons or companies and drilling earnestly every evening.

Practically every day from the commencement of the parades short exhortations were made by Mr. Browning to those present, urging them, where their circumstances would at all permit, to enlist in " Kitchener's Army," and shortly after its inauguration General Sir Bryan T. Mahon, who was then raising the Tenth (Irish) Division, visited the Corps and made a strong appeal for recruits.

Mr. Browning then got into touch with his old friend Lieutenant-Colonel Geoffrey Downing. He had been given command of the newly formed 7th (Service) Battalion of the Royal Dublin Fusiliers and had been well known in the football world in earlier years (1883) as captain of the first fifteen of Monkstown Football Club. Colonel Downing agreed to keep open a special company, " D " Company as it was subsequently known, for " Pals " from the Irish Rugby Football Union Volunteers, and there appeared in the daily press in the early part of September the following letter :

" *To the Irish Rugby Football Union Volunteers,*

"I am keeping my Battalion open for you to join. Come in your platoons (fifty men). ' Mess,' ' drill,' and work together, and, I hope, fight the common enemy together. The 1st City of Dublin Cadets are joining me as a body. I am waiting for YOU, but I cannot keep open long. Come at once, TO-DAY.

"(Signed) G. Downing (Lt.-Colonel)
" Commanding 7th (Service) Battalion R.D.F."

THE "PALS" LEAVING DUBLIN FOR THE CURRAGH

THE PALS

Following up this appeal there appeared in the *Irish Times* of September 11 a spirited article encouraging the Volunteers to enlist. By September 12 eighty-nine had enlisted, and on September 14, in the same paper, Colonel Downing wrote as follows :

" I went to Lansdowne Road on Thursday afternoon, where Mr. Browning, the President of the Irish Rugby Football Union, gave me the opportunity of addressing the members of the Association who had volunteered for active service. After speaking to them for a few minutes they all, with one accord, elected to join the 7th Royal Dublin Fusiliers, and a more splendid set of young men I have hardly ever seen. With this advance guard of really true-hearted volunteers I can see in the very near future the makings of one of the finest battalions that Ireland has ever produced, and I feel a proud man to have the honour of commanding them."

The Colonel's efforts gave a great stimulus to the recruiting movement, and in a few days twenty or thirty more had joined, to be increased week by week by many others whose enlistment had been delayed for one reason and another. They all came under the command of Colonel Downing at the Curragh, and until August 15, 1915, when he was wounded at Kizlar Dagh. Although this is the history of the rank and file, one may quote of him the lines written of another great soldier :

> " *A good grey head which all men knew,*
> *A voice from which all men their omens drew,*
> *An iron nerve to each occasion true,*
> *A tower of strength*
> *That stood four square to all the winds that blew.*"

THE PALS AT SUVLA BAY

With the names of Mr. Browning and Lieutenant-Colonel Downing there is another that may be mentioned without making any invidious distinction.

Sergeant-Major Guest, D.C.M., will ever be a name to conjure with where there are any of the " D " Company forgathered. When the " Pals " entered as Volunteers at Lansdowne Road he came to train them, and it was there they first heard his sharp well-trained words of command which demanded a prompt response. He went with them to the Curragh as their Company Sergeant-Major. On the voyage to the East he was made Regimental Sergeant-Major, and in the summer of 1916 he received at Salonika a commission in his old battalion. He had been with them all the time, always counselling and encouraging, whether under shrapnel and rifle fire at Suvla or among the snows of the Balkans. He was proud of them and they were proud of him, as of all their leaders, whom nothing but the best would please. His strong personality, splendid courage, and rare common sense made him at all times of difficulty a host in himself. His greatest reward has been, not his well-won D.C.M. or his commission, but the goodwill, admiration, and friendship of every one, from private to officer, who ever came in contact with him.

CHAPTER II

THE CURRAGH

ON Wednesday, September 16, 1914, those who had up to that date enlisted from the Corps, 110 in number, left Dublin via Kingsbridge for the Curragh to enter upon their military training. They marched off from the headquarters of the Dublin University O.T.C., where they had been paraded. What class of men were they? Barristers, doctors, solicitors, stockbrokers, bankers, medical students, engineering students, art students, business men who had responsible positions, civil servants, insurance agents, and many others of a similar class—the best that Dublin City could give, and nearly all of them men well known in its public and social life. In their march through College Green, Dame Street, and the Quays to the station they received a great ovation from the public and their friends. From almost every window in Nassau Street, College Green, and Dame Street handkerchiefs and hands were waved to them.

They arrived at the Curragh about 5 p.m., in heavy rain, and when paraded in front of the barracks received a short " welcome " address from Colonel Downing. " D " Company, the " Pals," were then put into their quarters in " C " Block of the Gough Barracks, in which their first meal as Tommies was taken—tea, in pails, with loaves and jam. Although in new surroundings, most of them admitted afterwards that they slept soundly the first night under the military roof.

On parade the next day in the forenoon they were again

addressed by Colonel Downing, who pointed out to them briefly the main duties of soldiers so far as discipline, conduct, and the honour of the regiment were concerned. After this, on the same day, they were inoculated against typhoid, a process which did not entail much inconvenience. During the next few days they were directed to elect from among themselves men to be non-commissioned officers, and also to elect two from among their number to be commissioned as their officers. For the latter positions they selected Ernest Julian, a barrister and professor of law in Trinity College, a man of high character, much learning, and strong individuality, and R. G. Douglas, who had been known to most of them in sport.

During the first week or ten days they enjoyed immensely the drill on the sunny mornings of September. The first military pay was received by them on the memorable date of September 25, and many were the humorous scenes and discussions as to how it would be spent. Some of them kept it as a memento and marking the first stage of their career.

The end of the month was reached before the regimental numbers were given to them and their uniforms and puttees supplied. During this period their principal exercises, in addition to the formal parades, were the Swedish drill and steeplechases. Many a double they had round Donnelly's Hollow, a well-known field which takes its name from the Irishman—Dan Donnelly—who won a prize-fight on this spot on October 13, 1815, against an Englishman named Cooper from Staffordshire.

In the month of October the drill went on with much vigour. They were all recommended to study " Infantry Training " and make themselves proficient in its precepts. To help them on the route marches they organized among themselves a mouth-organ band, which turned out a great success.

THE CURRAGH

During October Captain Harrison, formerly of the 51st Sikhs, succeeded Major Loudon in command of "D" Company, and as they grew to know him better at the Curragh, at Basingstoke, and later on at Suvla, the whole company gave him their loyalty, respect, and affection. Many letters from the "Pals" after his death, on the morning of August 16, 1915, showed how deeply affected they were, and how they loved him as a man and as an officer.

Snow began to fall in November, and any one who knows the Curragh can believe that it is a bleak and cheerless spot with the snow on the ground. About the end of this month the ordinary routine of drill, route marches, and Swedish exercises was varied by the introduction of the company to the intricacies of musketry training and the more laborious work of making trenches. Two notable events about this time were a brigade night attack and a brigade route march. About four thousand men were engaged in the brigade night attack and they extended and carried out operations almost to Kildare, and some of the "Pals" wrote home that it was rather trying work having to kneel or lie down in the cold night for cover when they were halted, and then suddenly, when properly stiff, having to rise and double a considerable distance. How little this would have troubled them later on ! This so-called inconvenience was not even mitigated by permission to smoke or talk. The brigade route march was one in which four battalions, the 6th and 7th Royal Dublin Fusiliers and the 6th and 7th Royal Munster Fusiliers, took part. They marched from the Curragh to the Hill of Allen with full kit and equipment. It was the most arduous march up to this point, but later on would have been regarded as a trifle.

For training in attack and defence from trenches they were taken to a set of model trenches which had been made by the engineers about two miles from the barracks, and here they had frequent practice which must have been of great service to them in the following year at Suvla Bay. About this time they began also to get what is called " company training."

In the beginning of December the Machine Gun Section for the battalion was formed, for which a picked lot of men were taken from " D " Company. They were put under the command of Second Lieutenant Douglas and Sergeant Weatherill, both from the " Pals," and the section was transferred to " B " Company. Though they were thenceforth nominally " B " and on the pay-roll as such, they always looked on themselves as " Pals " with " D " men, and when possible were always with them. The names of those transferred were : Douglas, R., Second Lieutenant ; MacDonald, C. J.; Brett, J. T.; Clarke, J. R.; Crookshank, H.; Dodd, F. J. ; Exshaw, R. L. ; Falkiner, F. E., Corporal ; Frazer, D. M. ; Houston, T. ; Weatherill, E. T., Sergeant ; Jenkins, C. E. ; Keesham, M. J. ; Scott, A. ; Shanagher, D. P. ; Marrable, F. A. ; Mathews, W. ; Murray, A. H. ; McFerran, W. R., Lance-Corporal ; Roberts, H. ; Thompson, F. R. ; Tait, W. ; Young, W.

Another event of interest at this period was that Poole Hickman, one of themselves, a man of great determination and ability, who had been a successful barrister on the Munster Circuit, was gazetted a full lieutenant and in his own company, of which he, in January 1915, obtained the captaincy.

On the morning of December 5 they left the camp for Dublin and Woodbrook, where they were to be entertained by Lieutenant Stanley Cochrane, and the return journey, begun on the morning of the 7th, was the occasion of their memorable route march from Dublin to the Curragh.

They came by train to Kingsbridge Station, where they arrived on the Saturday morning, and marched through the City by the Quays, Dame Street, Nassau Street, Merrion Square, Northumberland Road, Ballsbridge, and along Anglesea Road to Donnybrook. They received along the whole line of march a great and enthusiastic reception from their old friends and the citizens generally. One could easily see, as they passed, the splendid benefit they had all gained from the four months' strict military training at the Curragh. From Donnybrook they went by the Stillorgan Road to Woodbrook, where they arrived at 2.30 p.m. During the afternoon and evening they were royally entertained by their host at both dinner and tea. A smoking concert was held in the evening, and amongst other items they had a short and encouraging address from the Colonel, complimenting them on the way they had faced the training and benefited by it. Church parade was the principal incident on Sunday forenoon, and before dinner the ubiquitous photographer appeared and took the four platoons one by one. They were allowed to spend the afternoon and evening with their friends in the neighbourhood or in Dublin.

Réveillé on Monday morning the 7th brought them a soft, grey dawn with the prospect of a fine day for their long march over the mountains. The company breakfasted at 6.30 a.m., and an hour later marched off by Little Bray and the Dargle, past Enniskerry Bridge and through Powerscourt Demesne. Perhaps none of the company had ever before been in Powerscourt Demesne in the early morning, or had ever realized the beauty of the splendid panoramic views that were disclosed as they marched along. They passed out of the demesne by the far gate and proceeded up the valley to Glencree. The band of the Glencree Reformatory came about a mile down the road to meet them and played them up to the school, where they were hospitably entertained for an hour, leaving at 12.15 p.m. They then marched along the mountain road to Sallygap, past Liffey

Head and Coronation Plantation, and when evening came they moved along in the darkness, reaching Blessington about six o'clock, all very tired after the day's march of twenty-seven miles.

At Blessington they were billeted in Downshire House, which was then empty, and, having cooked some stewed meat and potatoes in their billy cans, lay down to sleep on the boards.

They were awakened by réveillé at 5.30 a.m. on the Tuesday morning, and left about 8.30, making towards the Curragh. When some miles from Blessington they raised a cheer at seeing the Curragh Water Tower many miles away in front of them.

They went through Ballymore Eustace, past Stonebrook and Kilcullen, outside which village they lunched on brawn sandwiches and cold sausages, supplied through arrangements made by their host of the week-end with a Dublin caterer.

At 1.30 p.m. lunch was over and they then took up the portion allotted to them in divisional manœuvres, which were then being carried out from the direction of the Curragh.

" D " Company acted as the advance guard of a brigade, and very soon met " B " Company, which formed the rear guard of another brigade. The advance guard engaged " B " Company in action, and as they approached the Curragh near Athgarvan, the General and some of his Staff were out to see how " D " Company—the chosen of Dublin—would acquit themselves in the final stages of the mimic battle, after their trying experiences over the mountains and from Blessington. They chased " B " Company half-way across the Curragh, under the eyes of the General, who was quite pleased with their fitness and freshness at the end of their manœuvres. It was their first severe trial and they stood it well.

It would appear that after the Bray march Captain

AT THE CURRAGH

A REST ON A ROUTE MARCH

A GROUP AT THE ROYAL BARRACKS

COMPANY SERGEANT-MAJOR GUEST

COMPANY QUARTERMASTER-SERGEANT
MYLES, COMPANY SERGEANT-MAJOR
GUEST, AND SERGEANT W. ATKINSON

A GROUP AT THE ROYAL
BARRACKS

Harrison contracted a chill, which brought on an attack of rheumatic fever from which he was *hors de combat* for several months. This was a great loss to the company.

We may here opportunely give an extract from a letter written to a friend about the officers of the company by Colonel Downing after his return from Suvla. He said :

" Captain Harrison's severe illness had been a terrible loss to the company—he had brought them on in a wonderful way. They admired and loved him and would have followed him anywhere. I was at my wits' end to find a suitable substitute, but I eventually decided to put Lieutenant Poole Hickman temporarily in command. My choice was justified, as he took to his job like a duck to the water and was a remarkable example of how our country produced at that period efficient amateur officers to fill the gaps in the Regulars, although they had little or no previous military knowledge. Shortly afterwards, in consequence of his good work, I was able to promote him to the rank of captain and to the permanent command of " D " Company, which position he held until his death leading them into action. He was a hard-working, clever, brave officer, always considering the welfare of his company. His was no mean task to fill the place of Captain Harrison, but he was ably supported by the other officers in the company. Captain Tobin (Paddy), his second in command, was one of the most splendid young officers I have ever known. His work seemed to come to him naturally and he was brave and fearless to a degree. The subalterns of the company, Lecky, Hamilton, and Crichton, by their untiring hard work and energy also gave him the greatest assistance.

" They were all worthy commanders of the splendid men they eventually led into action."

THE PALS AT SUVLA BAY

Two more heavy brigade route marches came in before the Christmas leave was granted on December 14. There was heavy snow at this time, which made the marching very irksome.

On Christmas Day those who were in barracks had a Church parade, and later on a smoking concert. In the afternoon " C " Company's pipes and drums played up and down in front of the barracks. On the 28th, a few days after Christmas, most of the " Pals " will remember a great snowball fight with the Munsters, resulting in no casualties, but in several windows of the barracks being broken.

With the beginning of the New Year they found one of their number, Lieutenant Stanley Cochrane, created a baronet. About this time the battalion training began in its various forms, and long route marches and severe night operations were very frequent. This brought them up to the end of January, during which there had been many rumours as to what would be their next destination.

While they were at the Curragh they were visited by the famous " D." of the Dublin *Evening Mail*, who gave with his inimitable pen the following description of what he saw and heard :

" I paid a visit to the Curragh yesterday and watched the recruits of the 7th Battalion of the Royal Dublin Fusiliers at the labour of love and loyalty that they have undertaken, in striving in the shortest possible time to become, as the official Laureate of the Empire puts it, men that are ' handled and made.' And they are succeeding very rapidly indeed.

" I was particularly interested in ' D ' Company, the ' Footballers,' as they were known when they were first drafted to the Curragh. The title is steadily drifting into abeyance. They were footballers when they went to the

A CURRAGH GROUP

A GROUP AT STRAFFAN

FROM LEFT TO RIGHT : CAPT. CUNNINGHAM, LIEUT. BELL, CAPT. LUCIE-SMITH, CAPT. FITZGIBBON, LIEUT. HAMILTON, LIEUT. LECKY, CAPT. POOLE HICKMAN

SOME MACHINE-GUNNERS

TRENCH-DIGGING

CHAP. II

NO. 13 PLATOON

"D" COMPANY LEAVING THE ROYAL BARRACKS
CAPTAIN POOLE HICKMAN LEADING

COLONEL DOWNING, MAJOR HOLY (ADJT.),
AND MAJOR LONSDALE

THE REGIMENTAL MASCOT, "JACK"

THE MACHINE-GUN SECTION

AT THE ROYAL BARRACKS

CHAP. II

Curragh. They are soldiers of the King now ; and proud to be nothing else ; and, above all, proud to be serving in the ' Old Toughs.'

" I watched them at their drill in Gough Square vicinity ; and they went through their movements with splendid precision and confidence. It was difficult to believe that the majority of the men were civilians like the rest of us only a month ago. They marched and countermarched, and formed fours ; and wheeled and counterwheeled, and deployed and performed all the other evolutions of the parade ground with, so far as I could judge, the smartness and certainty of veterans. The Prussian drill-sergeant is supposed to be the last word in efficiency production. No cursing, swearing, jack-booted, bullying Prussian non-commissioned officer could have his men in better shape or fitness.

" I am not going to say that in this case, as they say before the footlights, it is all done by kindness. It is all done by keenness. Men, non-commissioned officers and officers are all animated with the one desire : to do credit to the regiment ; to get on with the business in hand ; and then to get to the Front. They have to work very hard. They are at it before breakfast and again before dinner, and again before tea. They seemed to me to be gluttons for work, and more work, and harder work. The labour they delight in physics pain.

" I saw them again, after dinner—and they have their dinner at one, and are at work again at two—marching out to the veldt of the Curragh, and practising the great war game. In half an hour you see them dotted in detachments across the plain. Over there to the left men are practising signalling. In front of you a platoon is marching away and gradually opening out their line, as you would stretch an elastic band. They are advancing in extended order. Others are scouting towards the wood on the horizon, dropping behind cover and progressing by short rushes. Others again are lying in a saucer-like hollow in the grass and practising rifle-drill for the future work in the trenches. They are getting hard as nails, busy as ants, and keen as mustard.

" Keenness means efficiency, and efficiency means the Front, with interludes of promotion. And promotion is quick in Kitchener's Army, though not everybody wants it. I met a non-commissioned officer who, one of his comrades told me, had twice been offered a commission and was still in the non-commissioned ranks. They all can't get commissions in their own corps, and some don't seem to want it in any other. Thus is the *esprit de corps* tried and tested.

" Promotion, as I say, is quick in Kitchener's Army to those who merit it. In the interval between dismiss and dinner I was taken into the men's recreation-room, with a billiard-room on one side and a general room on the other. A soldier came forward to greet me. His name was Atkinson. The last time I saw him he was wearing a wig and gown in the Four Courts. He has since been promoted to the rank of lance-sergeant.

" In the Officers' Mess, a comfortable building, with an entrance hall decorated with trophies of the chase, and a fine messroom on one side and an equally fine dining-room on the other, the first ' Old Tough ' I came across was Lieutenant Poole Hickman. The last time I met him he, too, was wearing a wig and gown. He, too, had been promoted to another battle-ground. Then I came across Lieutenant Julian, formerly Reid Professor of Law in Dublin University, and a member of the Irish Bar. He also had been promoted to the Irish Brigade.

" He was engaged on an inspection of the men's boots before lunch. One might ask, alas, what boots it with incessant care to inspect the footwear of Thomas Atkins ? Lieutenant Julian, fresh from inspecting the oiling process, could give you the answer. Then I came across Lieutenant

Stanley Cochrane, of Woodbrook. He is, if I mistake not, His Majesty's Lieutenant for County Wicklow. He has now worked his way up to be a lieutenant in the Dublin Fusiliers bound for the Front.

"Lieutenant Fitzgibbon told me that he was feeling very fit and enjoying the work. The last time I saw him was in the lobby of the House of Commons, talking to his father, Mr. John Fitzgibbon, M.P., the well-known member of the Irish Party. Soldiers, of course, have no politics, and we pretermitted our accustomed discussion on Home Rule. Then I came across Captain De Montmorency, whom I last met when he was an inspecting officer of the Irish National Volunteers. Captain De Montmorency, who has seen a good deal of service, told me how very pleased he was with the men. If I am any judge, he has good reason to be.

"The men are well fed, well led, and well housed, and as pleased as Punch with their new life. Private Findlater, one of the two well-known brothers who have joined the corps, and whom I met at the station, gave me a cheerful account of the cordial relations between the men, and of the respect and regard that are entertained for the officers. Under Colonel Downing, who, I hear, may be induced to authorize an Irish terrier for a regimental mascot, the 7th Battalion of the Royal Dublin Fusiliers is becoming already a fine regiment. It will soon be a picked regiment. When it goes to the Front, as I believe it will do in a couple of months, it will carry the confidence as well as the good wishes of the class and territory it will worthily represent."

It is a soldier's privilege to "grouse."

Coming out of civilization and living under conditions intended to produce a man of war, he has a poor imagination who cannot see many things to "grouse" about, but at the Curragh there was always somebody ready to exclaim, when work and parades were incessant and grumbling was flying around : "Never mind, lads. The more duty, the more honour."

During one of the marches from the Curragh, the men were much amused by an old lady, who thoughtfully watched them march past her cottage near the Curragh at the end of their long tramp. She was evidently studying them and thinking of the job they were training for. What she meant no one knew, but she exclaimed to herself : "God help you, boys."

By this time they all longed for a turn of training in Dublin. Their wishes were gratified when on February 2, 1915, they were transferred to the Royal Barracks, Dublin, where what was called "the hard grind" was put upon them. Not a day's rest was given them. They were marched out on long journeys with full kits in all weathers. Manœuvres were carried out on the Dublin mountains, and once they slept, dog-tired, in the snow at Stepaside. They will never forget Flanagan's Quarries and the hard toil they experienced in stamping on them, day after day, the devices of the 7th Dublins in the form of trenches. By night and by day they built and occupied them, and weary work it was.

During the last month of their stay at the Royal Barracks there were many rumours prevalent as to when and where they were going, but the departure came suddenly on April 30, when they marched through Dublin to North Wall, having the special privilege of the Territorial regiment to march with fixed bayonets. One cannot do better than reproduce the stirring description of their departure which appeared in the *Irish Times* of the day following :

" The departure of the 7th Battalion Royal Dublin Fusiliers from their headquarters, Royal Barracks, Dublin, for completion of training was the occasion of a great public demonstration yesterday. The formation of the battalion has aroused much interest, as it was generally known as 'The Pals' Battalion.' From all classes of the community men came forward readily in defence of the Empire, and from all quarters of the city, from the fashionable centres and from the slums of the city, able-bodied citizens flocked to the Colours, and the scenes of enthusiasm that were witnessed yesterday proved that the city pulsates with ardent enthusiasm for the cause of the Allies. The fact that in the battalion was included the famous 'D' Company, mainly comprised of footballers, lent additional interest to the departure. The company includes within its ranks, barristers, solicitors, and other representatives of the professions, in addition to civil servants and bank officials, and it is naturally regarded as being typical of the spirit that animates the country as a whole. Its composition is symbolical of the part that sport plays in war. Men who were prominent in the football field, and whose prowess was admired every Saturday at Lansdowne Road and other football centres, have thrown aside their interest in sport and devoted themselves purely to the affairs of war, in order that Ireland and other parts of the Empire may be kept free from the horrors of war. Crowds lined the route yesterday, and the departure of the troops was accompanied by continuous cheering by dense lines of spectators."

The departure of the battalion from the Royal Barracks was timed at 3.30 p.m., and shortly before that hour the men were drawn up on parade on the square. Lieutenant-Colonel G. Downing, in command of the battalion, having inspected the lines, addressed the men and complimented them on their excellent behaviour during their stay in Dublin. He mentioned that the 1st and 2nd Battalions had already distinguished themselves at the front, and he felt sure that the men under his command would acquit themselves in a manner befitting the record of the " Dublins." The Germans had a song, " Deutschland über Alles," but their war-cry was, " Dublin over all." " Gott strafe England " was the motto of the enemy, but the Dublin Fusiliers would simply try to act up to their regimental motto, *Spectamur agendo*. Asked by a Press representative whether he had a message to send to the citizens of Dublin, Colonel Downing said: " We will do our best. Judge us by our deeds."

Relatives and friends crowded the square and bade farewell to those near and dear to them who were leaving all that was precious in life to face the attacks of the oppressor. Ladies of rank and women of humble degree moved through the lines, and gave parting gifts to their dear ones. A touching incident took place just before the battalion got into marching order. A man who had evidently fallen into ill-health, and who had served with the battalion until he was discharged, approached Colonel Downing and wished him and the battalion God-speed. He hoped that they would come safely back, and he was sorry that circumstances prevented him from taking his place in the battalion. Headed by the band of the 12th Lancers, and the pipers of the Officers' Training Corps, Trinity College, the battalion moved out of barracks. As they emerged through the main entrance they were cordially cheered, and the cheers were taken up all along the route. They looked exceedingly fit, and presented a fine military bearing. As they marched by in perfect order and in swinging, rhythmic step, every one felt that they were worthy of the city and of a country noted for its soldiers. The men were in great spirit, and laughed and joked along the way. The Union Jack and the Irish Flag were carried on the spikes of the bayonets, and wherever they were noticed cheers were raised. In addition to their heavy packs, some of the men carried melodeons strapped to their kit-bags.

30

THE CURRAGH

As they passed down the Quays, the crowd on the pavement and the occupants of windows lustily cheered, and the men, recognizing friends along the route, returned their farewell greetings with hearty cheers. In front of the Four Courts a large crowd of barristers, solicitors, and officials gave a cordial send-off to the men. Amongst the crowd were judges, whose sittings had concluded for the day, and they cheered as spontaneously as the others as the men passed. In the ranks were members of the Bar, who had forsaken excellent prospects to keep the Old Flag flying, and as they were recognized they were cordially cheered. In Dame Street and College Green, where flags were profusely displayed, crowds of spectators lined the thoroughfare, and gave vent to their feelings in frequent outbursts of enthusiasm. At O'Connell Bridge the crowd was particularly dense, and hats and handkerchiefs were waved on all sides. As the last stages of the march were reached the lines of spectators became more dense, and many touching scenes were witnessed. The significance of the occasion became more marked at this stage than heretofore. Fashionably dressed ladies walked beside their brothers and relatives, and women in shawls kept step with their husbands, brothers, and sons. The contrast was marked, but it served to show the spirit that animates the people. Men going to the Front under such conditions, with their minds set on one purpose, could be depended upon to act up to the glorious records of their regiment.

> " *Do you remember when they left ;*
> *The day they passed through town,*
> *And their bayonets flashed like a spray of steel,*
> *On a river of rolling brown ?* "

CHAPTER III

BASINGSTOKE

AFTER their triumphant march through the principal streets of Dublin, they were embarked upon a transport at North Wall—a passenger steamer which usually plied between Harwich and The Hook. Mr. Browning was the last man to leave the boat and wave " Good-bye— Good luck." They left North Wall at 6.40 p.m., and after a pleasant voyage reached Holyhead at 10.50 p.m. The transport was accompanied by two destroyers, and it was interesting to see their evolutions for the purpose of keeping the course clear. On the arrival of the transport at Holyhead, as the troop train had not arrived, the men stood about on the dock and pier until between one and two o'clock a.m., when they were entrained. They travelled through the night, via Birmingham, Warwick, and Oxford, to the now well-known town of Basingstoke, where they found they were to share the camp with the other units, about 15,000 men, making up the Tenth Division.

The camp looked very well in the sunlight—like a big white city—one half sloping down to the road and the other half upwards on the other side. The tents seemed new, and the whole place had an air of cleanliness and brightness. At first the inhabitants were somewhat stand-offish and, one would have thought, uncivil, and in the shops and restaurants seemed unwilling to have the custom of soldiers, but as time went on they rather melted in their manner. Their first attitude was due, it was said, to the fact that the pre-

32

decessors of the Tenth Division had been somewhat rough in their behaviour.

Their first night under canvas was on May 1, and as they were somewhat pressed for room, dressing, washing, and messing were a little awkward and inconvenient. Still, as the weather was glorious, few complained. As a rule there were about eleven in each tent. On the next morning they were all interested in seeing the first aeroplane that appeared over their camp, and the men could be seen standing in groups watching it, uncertain whether it was hostile or otherwise.

Every one could see that there was a spirit of keenness among the men, and there was much talk about how soon the whole division would be mobilized and moved off together, probably in a few weeks.

They came under the first experience of lighting restrictions, and under these orders no lights were allowed at nights and no noise or singing. When they had an opportunity of seeing what the country round them was like, they found it was pretty in a stiff, cultivated sort of way.

The training at Basingstoke consisted of heavy, long route marches, involving billeting schemes for days at a time, under war conditions of equipment and food, brigade and divisional manœuvres lasting for several days, and most exacting schemes of trench-digging by day and night—all of such a character that they put the severest strain upon the physique of our young soldiers. Some of the places visited on these marches and manœuvres were : Odiham, Hartley Row, Alton, Hartley Wespall, Upton Green, Newbury, and Aldershot. From each company there were chosen twenty-four men for special training in bomb-throwing, and when in camp or near it they went twice a day to Hackwood Park, the seat of Lord Curzon, where the training was carried out. During these manœuvres the food was good, but the provision for water was somewhat inadequate. Water-bottles could occasionally be filled from the regimental water-carts for drinking purposes, but there was little water for washing during the several days that the manœuvres lasted. It was no novelty during a long wait to see some of the men strip and bathe in a muddy ditch by the roadside. You would see them wash and shave in a puddle of rain-water, some of them even shaved with a portion of tea saved from breakfast, and a man has been known to wash with half the contents of a water-bottle poured into a mess-tin.

The first divisional manœuvres were held in the neighbourhood of Odiham, where the Tenth Division were to carry out an attack. They left Basingstoke on Wednesday, May 12, for Odiham, where they were to billet that evening before advancing to the attack the next day. Before leaving camp, each man got a piece of meat and some potatoes, from which he had to cook his dinner in his own mess-tin on arrival.

Here was the first experience of " D " Company in billeting. They were marched into an old school, at least as many of them as could get into it, and those who could not had to sleep in the open. Each man had his waterproof sheet and a blanket. In the middle of the night those who were sleeping in the open awakened to find themselves being drenched by the heavy rain which came on.

Réveillé sounded at 4.30 a.m. on Thursday morning, and they started off in the rain, with the prospect of fighting all day and bivouacking in a field or wood that night. The fight was started, but owing to the incessant downpour all day it was given up in the evening and the troops were ordered to march back to Basingstoke, a distance of ten miles. This march long remained in the memories of " D " Company, and some of them showed signs of distress, but none fell out before Basingstoke was reached, after four hours' dreary trudging over the flooded roads. To make matters worse, the camp and tents were in an appalling condition of mud and wet. Most of the men went to bed immediately on their arrival, as they had no dry clothes to put on, their overcoats being completely soaked, as, indeed, was all their clothing. The overcoats were sent away to be dried, but they had to make the best shift they could to dry the rest of their clothing. That this might be accomplished, no one was asked to get out of bed until ten o'clock next morning, and the few that did get up were strange sights walking about wrapped up in a blanket. It also took them a long time to get rifles thoroughly and carefully cleaned.

Their condition when they returned to Basingstoke after this march is described as follows :

"We had no change of clothes, so we all lay about in blankets. We have no parade this morning as all our clothes are away now being dried. The costumes of the fellows are too wonderful. I have just been down to see the adjutant, who did not know me in my kit—trousers rolled up above the knees, no socks, and a woollen muffler round my head for a cap."

About May 18 they started more divisional manœuvres, during which they were billeted at Hartley Row, "D" Company and another being put into an empty house in fairly good condition, where they were very comfortable. It had two floors above the ground floor, with a lot of small rooms, and, strange as it may appear, held two companies —over five hundred men and officers. Of course all that was required was room for each man to lie down, and that with pretty close packing. The men were allowed to light fires in the grates to help with their cooking, which was a great blessing. They were roused early the next morning by

réveillé at 5 a.m., but as the brigade in which the " Dublins"
were was in reserve, it did not move off until 9 o'clock.
They came into action about 11 a.m., and fought for three
of four hours, mostly from the woods, against the Twelfth
Division, which consisted of English regiments. They then
marched back for dinner, which each man had to cook for
himself at the billets, which were reached about 5 o'clock,
the men having had nothing since breakfast at 6.30 a.m.
Having had dinner they marched back to camp at Basingstoke,
which was reached about 9 o'clock. It was a long day, but
the men slept well that night, as their packs had been on
for twelve hours, and they had been up for fifteen and a
half hours.

The next weekly divisional training took them first of all
to Hartley Wespall, for which they started about 6 a.m.,
réveillé having been at 3.30. The weather at this time was
tropical, and the heat intense, and they moved out at this
hour so as to march in the cool of the morning. They got
to their destination about 9 a.m., piled arms in a field and were
allowed for a time to laze about. Later in the day tropical
rain came down. The only buildings near that would afford
protection were a large barn and schoolhouse, which would
hold two companies. The usual toss of the coin decided
which two companies would sleep in or out. " D " Company
got the schoolhouse, and the other companies which were to
sleep out got the oil-sheets, but the rain did not continue.
The schoolhouse was only meant to hold thirty to fifty
children, and as they put 160 men and equipment in there
was a little crush. As the rain kept off, only seventy slept
in the school, and the remainder were allowed to sleep under
bushes and trees around the place. Those who were outside
had the advantage, as there were only three or four small
windows in the school for ventilation. For two days after
that they were up each morning at 3.30 a.m., marching

A BATHE AT BASINGSTOKE

A GROUP AT BASINGSTOKE

PREPARING FOR THE EAST

THE RANGE-FINDERS

AFTER THE BATHE

SERGEANT-MAJOR GUEST AND "D" COMPANY, AFTER THE INSPECTION

READY FOR THE EAST

HAIRCUTTING

NO. 14 PLATOON

READY FOR THE EAST

and manœuvring from 6 o'clock in the morning until 7.30 or 8 o'clock at night, and bivouacking in the open. This continued until Saturday morning at 9 o'clock, when they started to march back to Basingstoke. The following description of the long tramp is given by one of " D " Company :

" When we got half-way we felt the need of something to eat, although we had saved the evening ration of bread, a tin of rabbit, and some butter, but we did not get the chance to eat it, as the halts were only for ten minutes each hour. The bread was the only thing we could eat, as it could be chewed while marching. You know, on the march we are not supposed to accept any eatables or drink from people, but at one halt a lady had a big enamel jug of milk, of which our captain had a good long pull. We did not know that it was milk until we marched by the house. At the next halt a lady had a jug of home-made ginger-beer, so, as I was not going to be done out, I asked permission of our sergeant to have some. He said I could go when the sergeant-major went, so immediately he went I followed like a shadow and had a fine drink, but shortly afterwards nearly the whole platoon swarmed over. When we got within two miles of our camp, I, in any case, was nearly beaten. The muscles of my thighs were simply worn out. I never experienced anything like it before, and, in fact, all the other fellows were in much the same state. While most of the fellows out of our tent went into town for a good feed, I and a fellow called Pennefather made our bed, which, in our opinion, would serve us better than a good feed. Needless to say we did not rise until 7 o'clock the next morning and felt much better then."

It was said that the course of training, which took them

three days a week out of the town itself, was adopted by reason of the scarcity of the water-supply, which was reported to be sufficient only to accommodate the troops for four days out of every week.

Here is a description of how some of their few spare moments at Basingstoke were occupied :

"C—— and M—— are sitting on the grass smoking and waiting for P——, who is an expert poacher. We have found a pool with some fine four- or five-pound trout in it, and we are going to try and get one or two to grace our homely board. So far we have spent most of our evenings here searching for food (bacon and eggs) in the town. It is next to impossible, as there are such a lot of men, but so far I have been fairly lucky. I also had the good fortune to meet a Dublin man called C——, who has given me leave to have a hot bath at his house any time I like. I only hope he won't get sick of the sight of me."

It was about this time that the severest musketry tests were imposed upon the battalions for the purpose of selecting picked marksmen as snipers. Twelve were taken for this purpose from the 7th Battalion Royal Dublin Fusiliers, and the same number from each of the other battalions.

One of the company describes the route march on Whit Monday, 1915, as the most tiring he can remember. Their destination was Aldershot, whither they were bound for field firing. It was a broiling hot day, and they began to feel the pace towards noon. As they trudged along, weary, footsore, and heavy laden, they could not help thinking of previous Whit Mondays spent at Baldoyle Races, sports at Ballsbridge, or perhaps whipping the streams near Dublin. They halted for a rest on the outskirts of Aldershot, covered with dust and wet with perspiration. Some of the boys lamented not joining the Flying Corps instead of a " foot-slogging regiment." Others in a tired but devout voice said, " God send peace." Some there were who said nothing at all, but conjured up visions of many long drinks. Eventually they discovered their tents situated on a sandy plain. The fine sand got into everything, including the inevitable stew for dinner. But before dinner there was a wild stampede in the direction of the canteen. The men were afflicted with overwhelming, perfectly irresistible thirsts and clamoured loudly for refreshment. To cope with such a thirst the company sergeant-major turned barman for the time being and helped to dispense the cheerful liquid. In the evening they had thoroughly recovered, and, their work being over, they repaired to the town of Aldershot, which was thronged with soldiers of every possible description, including stalwart gunners and lively little drivers of the Army Service Corps, smart-looking cavalry men and sober-looking men of the Royal Army Medical Corps.

On the morning of Saturday, May 28, the entire division marched to Hackwood Park to be inspected by the King, being drawn up in a huge hollow square. About 12 o'clock the King arrived, mounted and dressed in the uniform of a General. The Queen and Princess Mary followed him in a motor. As he rode into the square the buglers sounded the " Royal Salute," and there burst forth from twenty thousand healthy throats three rousing cheers. He rode round the square inspecting the troops, after which they marched past. The motor cyclists came first, about fifty of them; then the large armoured motor-cars; then the infantry in columns of companies. The King expressed himself to the General as being greatly pleased with their appearance and fitness.

On June 1 they were inspected by Lord Kitchener,

39

an indication that they might soon be on the move. One of the troops wrote of this inspection :

> " The performance was just the same as when the King reviewed us (May 28), only that you could see that Kitchener was noticing everything and studying the sort of men (rank and file) that the Tenth Division was made of."

Another very trying march they had was to Newbury, in the middle of June, for divisional manœuvres. It seemed to be the hottest day of the year, with tropical heat even at dawn. The Division marched off at about 7.30 a.m., and before they had gone ten miles over one hundred men had fallen out. "D" Company created quite a record on this march. Some of the other battalions had something like one hundred each falling out from heat and exhaustion, while the whole of the 7th Royal Dublin Fusiliers had only eight casualties, and "D" Company went right through without a single fall-out. They were the only company in the battalion to do this, and as a result extra week-end passes were issued to them. The rule forbidding them to accept or buy food or drink on the march was felt rather badly on this day. Sometimes at the halts buckets of water or perhaps lemonade would be brought out for them, but they were not allowed to touch it. Carts of oranges and bananas had to be allowed to pass, even though the men were parched with thirst and the water in their bottles had got warm. The regimental water-carts were, of course, with them, but there was only a limited quantity permitted to each man.

They got into Newbury late in the afternoon, and after the usual delays tumbled into their billets. "D" Company got a store with a cement floor, and the men had nothing between themselves and its cold surface but the waterproof sheet. However, they were packed tight enough to be warm.

BASINGSTOKE

One advantage of this place was that those who wished were able that evening to have a swim in the public baths and a decent meal in the town. They went to bed thinking that réveillé was to be at 2.30 a.m., but the order was changed during the night and they had not to get up until 5 a.m., and after breakfast they marched off for the day's manœuvres. During that day the battalion never really got into the firing-line, though they marched by stages for many miles. They could only hear the field-guns and artillery in the distance.

A few of " D " Company, who were sent out to watch a particular portion of the country, got very hungry late in the evening, and were fortunate enough to find a cottager who gave them a large loaf of fresh bread, a pound of cheese, and a jug of gooseberry vinegar, all for the sum of one shilling. During the night there were more manœuvres which involved marching up to the top of the hill, a very steep climb which made it slow work. A heavy fog came down during the night and it was very difficult for the various platoons of the battalion to get into touch with one another. After they had been placed in position, about midnight, sentries were posted and the rest of the men allowed to fall asleep on the oil-sheets in full equipment and overcoats, with one blanket to cover them. The heavy fog continued all night, and one of the men who had heard that there was a field-kitchen near with tea, and went out with his mess-tin to get it filled, succeeded in losing his way and did not return until dawn. A very striking incident on this morning was that sometime before dawn the whole battalion was awakened by hearing hundreds of larks that had risen from the hill singing in the sky. About half-past six on the Saturday morning they reassembled and marched back to Basingstoke, a long and ardous march under a very hot sun.

Towards the end of June, Newbury was again the scene of an extensive trench-digging scheme which tried the men to the very utmost. The weather was still very hot and they had to march a distance of eighteen miles to the place on which it was intended they should camp, and near which the trench-digging scheme of the Division was to be carried out. The eighteen miles were very trying, and, unfortunately, when the troops stopped to cook their dinner about half a mile from the site of the camp, a violent thunder-storm broke and soaked them through. When they had reached the camping-ground they had to pitch their tents in the rain on the wet ground and sleep in their wet overcoats. Fortunately their blankets were dry, so no one was any the worse.

At 8 a.m. on Sunday morning they were taken out to the trench-digging and kept hard at it until 11 a.m. This was to avoid the exhausting part of the day. They then rested and had dinner and went at it again at six in the evening and continued until 4 o'clock on Monday morning. They began again at 8 a.m. on that day and stopped at 11 a.m. for an hour and a half, and when they got back to the trenches they did not leave their operations until half-past three on Tuesday morning, a continuous stretch of over eleven hours. Rest was allowed during the morning and forenoon of Tuesday, but the digging was resumed from 2.30 until 8 o'clock, when they were allowed to sleep. An early start was made on Wednesday, réveillé being at 3.30 a.m., after which they had to strike tents, roll blankets and ground-sheets, load everything on the transport wagons and be ready to move off at 6.30 a.m., when they marched straight for Basingstoke, arriving there at 1.30 p.m. While at the work of trench-digging it seemed a " killer " to all, but its effect was such that no one fell out on the march back, although many had done so on the previous Saturday.

Immediately after this Newbury outing there was nothing but excitement, as the rumour had gone abroad that they were bound for the Dardanelles. New drill clothes, pith helmets, etc., were served out, and they knew that their time had come, and that they were bound for the Near East to fight the Turks.

During these days of the first week of July 1915 there was little training, as all the time was taken up fitting themselves out and getting ready. It was said to be quite amusing to watch the efforts of the men to fix on, in the best and neatest manner, the pugaree which is worn on the pith helmet. Then there was the usual inspection and cleaning up of the camp. On Thursday, July 8, the rumours became more insistent as to when and how they were to leave England. The general opinion was that it would be from Liverpool, but this turned out to be wrong. When they got up on Friday morning, July 9, they received orders to hand their blankets into store and to make ready for departure. The day was spent drawing haversack rations and fixing up equipment.

The news got abroad through the town that they were at last going, and many of their friends came to see them and wish them God-speed and a safe return. At 9 p.m. that night the battalion marched off, the men all jolly and full of excitement, though many may have been really heavy at heart. They had no knowledge where they were going or from what port they were to sail. However, at 3.30 a.m. the train stopped at a station which they found to be Exeter, and through the generosity of some ladies they were provided with refreshments, fruit, and cigarettes. Being in Exeter, it was an easy guess that Devonport was their destination, and they arrived there at 5.15 a.m.

When leaving Basingstoke one man summed up their experiences thus :

" We scoured the country within a radius of twenty miles

—and scoured it nearly clean. We slept inside and outside all sorts of places, packed tight. We became noted for three o'clock a.m. réveillés. Nothing but the same over again would fully recall the toil of that ten weeks of hard "graft" with full pack. We listened to the nightingale and night-jar as we took trenches. We slept in the roadway under the full glare of the midday sun, and paid for it afterwards whilst trying to march. We have sucked pheasants' eggs in the woods while we fought, and cooked our captured rabbits afterwards. What we had experienced in the district made us cheer as we marched from the camp to Basingstoke railway station."

The Tenth (Irish) Division which left Basingstoke on this night consisted of : (1) The 29th Infantry Brigade : The 10th Hants, 6th Royal Irish Rifles, 5th Connaught Rangers, and 6th Leinsters, under Brigadier-General Cooper. (2) The 30th Infantry Brigade : The 6th and 7th Dublins and the 6th and 7th Munsters, under Brigadier-General Nicol. (3) The 31st Infantry Brigade : The 5th and 6th Inniskilling Fusiliers and the 5th and 6th Royal Irish Fusiliers, under Brigadier-General Hill, C.B., D.S.O.

The following artillery : 54th, 55th, and 56th Brigade of Royal Field Artillery, 57th Howitzer Brigade, and the 10th Heavy Battery.

It also included the following details : Three Field Companies Royal Engineers, Army Service Corps, 30th, 31st, and 32nd Field Ambulance, and 5th Royal Irish Regiment (Pioneers).

The Division was under the command of General Sir Bryan Mahon, C.B., K.C.V.O., D.S.O., a soldier of great experience and ability, who had seen service in India, Egypt, and South Africa. He was born in Co. Galway, and no more suitable General could have been selected for an Irish Division.

CHAPTER IV

THE VOYAGE TO THE EAST

ON the morning of Saturday, July 10, about 7 a.m., they embarked on board the liner *Alaunia* along with the 6th Royal Dublin Fusiliers, had breakfast on board at 8.30 a.m., but lay in the dock until half-past four that afternoon. During the day nearly every one on board was seen writing a short note or a post card home as to the departure, usually getting it posted by some one in the dockyard. As the liner was towed out of harbour it was saluted by the sirens of other craft and the cheers of the people on shore, which were responded to by the soldiers on board. She lay at the mouth of the harbour until late that night, when she left the shores of England under the escort of two destroyers, which accompanied her until about 10 o'clock the next morning, when they were well away from the French coast, and signalling the *Alaunia* a message, " God-speed and a safe return," the destroyers went back and left her to " paddle her own canoe."

In the matter of quarters on board " D " Company was rather unlucky, as they were placed right at the bottom of the ship, where it was very hot and stuffy. The other companies had the accommodation of the berths and cabins on the upper decks, which were very comfortable, but in the end " D " Company solved the difficulty by sleeping on deck during the beautiful nights as they were going towards Gibraltar and down the Mediterranean.

There was a good supply of hot and cold water on board,

and as salt-water baths were available they were also a luxury to the men. The food was very good and the variety a change from the routine army rations of the previous ten months. In fact the good food and sea air soon combined to make the men feel very fit indeed.

The usual daily round was : Réveillé about 6 or 6.30 a.m., breakfast at 7.30 or 8 a.m. From 9 until 11 a.m., physical drill, then bathing in the large canvas baths filled with sea water that were rigged up on the ship for them until one o'clock, or they lay about the deck in the sun, reading, writing, playing cards or other games as they wished. They then had dinner, afterwards lifeboat drill or rifle inspection. They were then finished for the day and left to their own devices. The more popular card games, including " House " and " Wheel and Anchor," both so well known in Dublin, were much in vogue during the evenings.

Once or twice a week they had a good concert on board, generally got up by Lieutenant and Quartermaster Byrne of the 6th Royal Dublin Fusiliers, who acted as master of ceremonies and obtained the services of some excellent artistic talent which was on board. At night one part of the transport became a regular Monte Carlo. At every table, and in every corner, there were groups of five or six, each group forming a " school " of its own, and in addition to the games already mentioned they could be seen playing almost every kind of game of chance. Again, night after night, those who were more quietly disposed would watch the unusually beautiful sunsets, the colour of which some of them thought unique in their brilliancy and tone, or they would watch the shoals of porpoises following the vessel in the moonlight.

Through the Bay of Biscay it was pretty rough, but on the whole the men weathered it well. On the Tuesday, when the sea had calmed, there was a great Marathon race twenty times round the deck in bare feet.

They reached Gibraltar at 2 a.m. on Wednesday morning, July 14, and at daybreak they sailed again. They had no sooner got in sight of the lighthouse as they approached the Rock than suddenly from every conceivable point searchlights began to play on them, and warships to signal to one another all over the place. A cruiser followed the *Alaunia*, searching her with a full light. They swept its powerful rays into every hole and corner of the ship and then drew alongside, and a voice through a megaphone inquired: "What vessel is that?" After some other inquiries they seemed satisfied with the identity of the transport and went off. The cruiser then began a most elaborate system of signalling to the other warships with the lamp Morse code, as well as to the headquarters on the Rock. Not content with this means of conveying information, the signalling was continued by siren blasts, which sounded weird in the deep darkness before dawn, but it made them all realize the true significance of war.

As the sun came well up in the sky, on their right they could see the greyish mountains of Africa, and on their left the southern shores of sunny Spain. Africa looked very barren and dry, while Spain looked much more habitable and inviting, the mountains seeming to sweep down to the sea through fertile valleys.

The houses and streets of the town were clearly visible, and every man on board seemed to realize that the importance of this fortress as the key to the Mediterranean could not be overestimated. As they left Gibraltar they passed a steamer full of Italian reservists going to do *their* bit for *their* country.

Immediately on entering the Mediterranean the men were ordered to change from their khaki service uniform into khaki drill and to put on their pith helmets. This was a great relief, as the heat had become intense and the sea seemed like a large lake—very calm and only disturbed by the screws of the liner as she moved along.

It was on the night of this day that they once more slipped out of sight of land, with the sea like glass, and by the light of the new moon they could see several sharks following them, rolling over and showing the white gleam of their bodies and opening their big mouths. Between Gibraltar and their arrival at Valetta in Malta on Saturday, July 17, nothing exciting happened, save a lifeboat drill which had to be gone through when the bugle sounded the alarm, a boxing competition, and the sudden approach on Friday evening of two destroyers which they thought might be German or Austrian. They made straight for the *Alaunia* at full speed and came right up alongside, but they turned out to be Italian and the sailors gave a cheer as they went by. It was a great relief, as every one on board was waiting to be blown up. This would have been unfortunate for the good steamship, which had seen hard work in the month of April at the Gallipoli Peninsula, where it had been her duty to pass to and from the shore under the enemy's fire.

The ship came into the harbour of Valetta about 6 a.m., and a grand sight spread before them. Lying just inside the breakwater they could see the harbour absolutely packed with ships of all sorts, including French cruisers and destroyers. Shortly afterwards a Red Cross boat from the Dardanelles, full of wounded Indian soldiers, came in. During the day the chief amusement was obtained from watching the little Maltese diving boys, who were marvellously skilful at bringing a penny up from the bottom of the sea, as well as the hawkers who swarmed round the ship in small boats selling cigarettes, sweets, fruit, silk handkerchiefs, scarves, soap, etc. The method of dealing was to send money down in a basket fastened to a piece of string, and up came

THE CAMP, BASINGSTOKE

H.M. THE KING AND GENERAL SIR B. MAHON
ON THEIR WAY TO INSPECT THE 10TH
(IRISH) DIVISION

THE DUBLINS' LINES, BASINGSTOKE

A DRUMHEAD SERVICE BY THE PRIMATE OF ALL
IRELAND TO THE 10TH (IRISH) DIVISION
AT BASINGSTOKE

THE 7TH ROYAL DUBLIN FUSILIERS MARCH PAST

THE INSPECTION OF THE 10TH (IRISH) DIVISION BY
LORD KITCHENER AT BASINGSTOKE

CHAP. III

the goods, after great bargaining, accompanied with a variety of gesticulations and a perfect babel of voices. Among the swarms of craft which came alongside was one having an awning on which was emblazoned: " My father was an Irishman." Its owner must have known that the Tenth Division was coming! He jabbered and clamoured for trade most of the day, and before long they had nicknamed him the " Wah-Wah " man.

They stopped long enough to enable some of the officers to get ashore, but left in the evening about seven o'clock, accompanied for a few miles by a British cruiser. As they left the island, one of the men remarked that it reminded him very much of the Isle of Man, but without the boarding-houses!

The next stop was at Alexandria, on Tuesday, July 20. On the intervening Sunday and Monday there was no excitement, save the admiration of the sunsets and the beautiful calm sea. The heat was so intense, even at night, that most of the men slept on deck and were never cold. After arriving in Alexandria the ship lay in the harbour until late in the evening, when she moved up close to the docks. What a strange, magnificent harbour!

It was full of huge steamships and many sailing vessels like those seen in Biblical pictures, with the triangular sails. The hawkers were again round the ship in dozens. They also saw lying up a large American steamer which had been taken as prize, having on board a cargo of petroleum for Germany. The first rumour was that the Division were going to land there and stay for a fortnight or three weeks, but this idea was soon abandoned when they saw that all the kit-bags with the heavy khaki uniform and the extra boots were landed and taken to the big Army Service Corps stores in the city.

On the next morning, however, Wednesday, July 21,

D

the men were taken on shore at 6.30 a.m. for a route march round the place for three hours. Every one enjoyed the change of exercise and they saw a good deal of the town and many natives. The march was first through the poorest part of the city, where the people seemed very interesting, and from this into the better-class quarter, where they heard for the first time the funny Eastern music, the Khedive's mounted band playing outside his palace. From that the troops passed into the European district with its beautiful hotels, gardens, and trees. One of the men describes the scene as follows :

" At Malta we got a glimpse of the East—here was the real thing. Natives of every conceivable hue were clustered round the boat in a variety of costumes. Many wore the voluminous ' bags ' and fez, others wore European clothes, others long flowing garments of cotton such as religious men wear, and others as little as they possibly could. But such a riot of colour ! Every garment seemed to differ from its neighbour, red, purple, yellow, green, and grey were all mingled together. Pennies were flung overboard to the quays, and men, boys, and girls scrambled for them. Then, suddenly, where a moment ago had been good humour, the temper of the East showed itself—a row started suddenly, and in a moment sticks, stones, chunks of coal and blocks of wood, shovels and so forth were commissioned for the fray. Such noise ! Such confusion ! It was a little hell in itself ! A few coloured policemen came on the scene, lashed indiscriminately around with their canes, and in a few seconds order was restored. Then came the jugglers, performing marvellous feats. Swords were swallowed, nails driven into the nose and different parts of the body with apparent ease—and no trouble to the operator."

THE VOYAGE TO THE EAST

There was a very dusky boy of about eight years of age on the quay at Alexandria, who had a marvellous knowledge of rifle drill. He was given all sorts of words of command from the soldiers on the boat, but could not be tricked into doing anything wrong. He had evidently seen camp or barrack life.

On Thursday morning they heard the rumour that they were to leave that day for Lemnos, and as they went off in the evening about 6.30 o'clock it was blowing pretty hard and somewhat rough.

On Friday evening Crete or Candia came in sight, and the next day the ship passed through the Grecian Archipelago, arriving in Mudros Bay in the Island of Lemnos about six o'clock in the evening of Saturday, July 24. This was the naval base for the East, and full of all sorts and conditions of ships, big and small. Its entrance was protected by a double layer of torpedo-nets to safeguard the dozens of battleships, destroyers, mine-sweepers, liners, armed cruisers, hospital boats, trawlers, and pilot boats lying inside. They could see a few camps on shore, several wireless stations, heaps of stores, and the big lighthouse at the entrance.

Two torpedo boats were seen returning from a cruise in the Sea of Marmora and were greeted with great cheers from the warships for the work they had accomplished. Indeed the whole appearance of the harbour was evidence of Britain's sea-power.

There is a French camp at Mudros itself, and British camps dotted all over the place. The word "camp" does not necessarily imply tents, as there were very few of them, the "camps" merely being areas where men dumped their packs and lay down.

Some thought they were to stay here for some time, but just in the middle of church parade on the following day, Sunday, steam was got up and the *Alaunia* made a course

to the south-east from Lemnos, the news going around that
the 30th Brigade were to make for Mitylene, and in the afternoon a pilot came on board from a naval trawler to take them
through the narrow entrance into the land-locked harbour
of Port Hiero in the south-east corner of the Island of Mitylene.
At five o'clock p.m. they went through this entrance, which
was so narrow that they could nearly touch the hills on either
side as the ship passed up the neck of water into a beautiful
big bay. They thought the pilot was surely running them
aground as he steered his way between the hills—steep hills,
covered with olive groves, and rocks which swept down to
the sea. White-walled houses with red roofs were dotted
here and there like little hamlets over the sides of the hills.
There were about a dozen English and French battleships
anchored in the harbour and a searchlight played all night
for fear of submarines. A week later they were joined by
the 31st Infantry Brigade under Brigadier-General F. F.
Hill, C.B., D.S.O.

The *Alaunia* was the first transport ship to arrive there,
and the natives, who, as usual, came around the ships, were
very handsome Greeks with bronzed complexions, beautiful
curly hair, and fine features.

Mitylene is about 120 miles from Suvla, and the concentration there was possibly a feint with the object of drawing
the Turkish forces from the Peninsula. On arrival at Port
Hiero, maps and plans of Smyrna were distributed to the
officers with the same object, secrecy being ostensibly
enjoined. Officers were allowed to go ashore, being possibly
warned not to speak too much about the contemplated attack
on Smyrna! The Army Service Corps and other officers were
also landed on the island to select a site for a camp and a
depot for supplies. Negotiations were entered into with
various owners of land on the island for obtaining such a
depot, and a site was actually decided upon and carefully

planned. The place was known to be full of spies, and, as was expected, it was afterwards stated that these movements

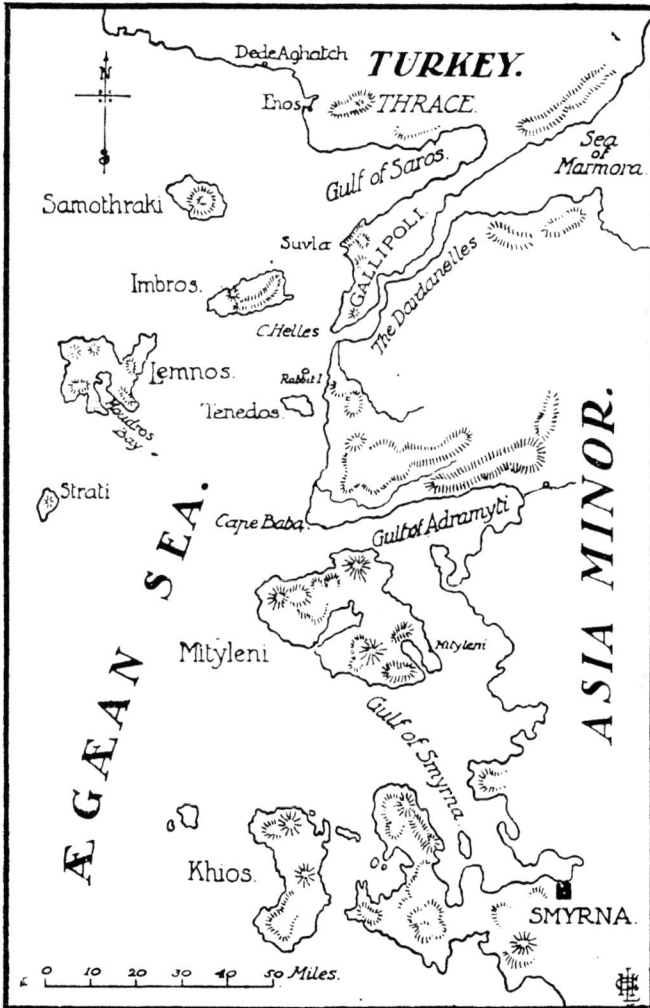

were faithfully reported to Turkish headquarters. There were now six battalions at Mitylene and they were placed under the command of Brigadier-General F. F. Hill, commanding the 31st Brigade.

THE PALS AT SUVLA BAY

While at Mitylene the troops were exercised by means of route marches round the bay. At first they landed without arms, but after some discussion with the Greek Governor and British representatives, they were afterwards allowed to land and march with rifles and a portion of their equipment. On these marches they took with them their various pipe bands, and going through the small villages caused much terror to the Turkish inhabitants, who fled to the hills, removing anything they could carry or drive—even the hens. On the other hand, they were received with great fervour by the Greeks, who took much interest in them. Both the Greek Civil and Military Governors of Mitylene were entertained by General Hill and officers on the *Andania*. The Military Governor especially was greatly taken with the appearance of the men, and frequently expressed his admiration for the " Fine Irish." The general idea was that the stay at Mitylene was to be prolonged until the attack on Smyrna could be properly organized, with Mitylene as a base, and acting on this assumption various entertainments to take place at the end of August were organized in honour of the troops by the Greek inhabitants. When the troops went on shore for marches they went from the transports on tenders and back on tenders.

They were there about a fortnight, during which the pleasantest occupation was bathing, either from the side of the ship or from the fishing boats, which they would take a considerable distance from the ship into the fresh, deep water, and some naturalists who reached the shore were interested to hear in the olive-trees the locusts making a funny noise like starlings. No bathing was allowed in the heat of the day, but only from six to eight o'clock in the morning and from five to seven o'clock in the evening.

On Thursday, July 29, the S.S. *Osmanieh*, a Khedival mail boat, came alongside to take the reserve back to Lemnos.

This meant, they thought, that the division was about to force a new landing.

The reserve consisted of fifty men picked from each company, and lots of " Pals " were separated there through their chums being put on the reserve list. Those who went were sorry to go, as they thought the others would be in the firing-line first, and those who were left were sorry to lose their friends, some of whom they never saw again.

These reserves who were left behind temporarily had not a very exciting time, but the excellent bathing at Mudros was very pleasant and they got plenty of it. They were at first put to make roads and then to erect hospital buildings. This indicated that something was going to happen on a pretty large scale in that district very soon, and they heard that covered-in accommodation for ten thousand patients was to be ready in fourteen days. This, of course, was impossible, and after some hospital huts had been erected tents were put up. They had, however, the advantage of their comrades at Mitylene, for on August 5 the first mails arrived. The orders to these reserves to proceed to Suvla were as sudden as at Mitylene. On August 6 they got unexpected orders to pack all equipment, each man to carry his rifle, ammunition, two days' iron rations, and his haversack. This meant that all he was to keep was what could be put into the little bag that hangs at the side of the soldier's equipment—not the big bag which goes at his back. Everything else was put inside a barbed-wire enclosure and left behind. The iron ration consisted of a white cotton bag with about a hatful of small biscuits, the size of an overcoat button, a small tin containing a cube of oxo, half an ounce of tea, and one ounce of sugar.

Meanwhile, for the remainder of the Division who had been left at Mitylene the routine of life was very much the same as at Mudros: a bathe before breakfast, after breakfast

COMMENCE AT 7.30 P.M.

CUNARD LINE

S.S. "ALAUNIA."

PROGRAMME OF CONCERT

HELD ON

H.M.T. "Alaunia,"

1st August, 1915.

BY KIND PERMISSION OF

COMMANDER A. H. ROSTRON, R.D. R.N.R.

COLONEL G. DOWNING,
Officer Commanding Troops.

LIEUT COL. P. A. G. COX,
Commanding 6th Royal Dublin Fusiliers.

Concert du Program

SUR

H.M.T. "ALAUNIA,"

LE PREMIER AOUT, 1915.

Par la permission cordiale de

M. le CAPITAINE A. H. ROSTRON, R.D., R.N.R.

M. le COLONEL G. DOWNING,
Officer Commanding Troops.

M. le COLONEL P. A. G. COX,
Commanding 6th R.D.F.

COMMENCE A SEPT HEURES ET DEMIE.

Programme

GLEE PARTY	H.M.S. "Euryalus"	Selected
SECOND-STEWARD CANTY, H.M.S. "Canopus"		Selected
PTE. HICKEY, 7th R.D.F.		Song
BELCHER, A.B., H.M.S. "Euryalus"		Selected
M. DELOR N de R.F "La Touche Travaille"		Song Selected
L-CPL. CONNOLLY & PTE. COLDWELL, 7th R.D.F.		Duet
MR. BYRNE, 6th R.D.F.		Song
GREEN, A.B., H.M.S. "Canopus"		Concertina Selection
PTE. HUNTER, 7th R.D.F.		Song
MR. BALLYN, H.M.T "Alaunia"		Song Selected
SERGT. CLARKE, 7th R.D.F.		Pianoforte Solo
PTE. SELFE "		Song
C Q M S KEATING, 6th R.D.F		Song
PTE COLDWELL, 7th R.D.F		Song
GUNNER W H WHITE, H.M.S. "Euryalus"		Song
L-CPL CONNOLLY, 7th R.D.F		Song
M. CAMOUS. N de R.P. "La Touche Travaille"		Song
STOKER JONES, H.M.S. "Canopus"		Song
E. R. A. NICHOL, H.M.S. "Euryalus"		Song
ROBERTS, A.B. "	"	Song
MR. HEALY, 6th R.D.F.		Song
DODD, A.B., "H.M.S. "Canopus"		Song

"LA MARSEILLAISE." "VIVE LA FRANCE."

"GOD SAVE THE KING."

drill and another bathe; then dinner and a short parade, then tea and the real "star" bathe of the day; while between the bathes and parades the men slept, read, or wrote their letters. The boat-loads of bathers were the best of fun. The men crowded into them with nothing but their towels around them, and many a scramble ended in some one going overboard. The boats, which carried fifty or sixty, went over to the bathing-place, and when the whistle blew brought them all back.

On the night of Sunday, August 1, they had a magnificent concert, entertaining about three hundred sailors from the French battleship, some of whom contributed to the programme, as did some of the sailors from the British warships round about.

On the morning of August Bank Holiday there was an inspection of the troops on the ships by General Sir Ian Hamilton and the General Staff.

The last route march they had was on August 4, when réveillé sounded at 3 a.m. They had breakfast at 4 a.m. in complete darkness, but as dawn comes very suddenly it was bright, broad daylight before breakfast was finished. The battalion boarded a big steam launch, were landed on the shore, went for a march across the outside part of the island, and saw Asia Minor in the distance for the first time.

The transport ships in Port Hiero during this period were :

Andania : Headquarters 31st Infantry Brigade, 6th Royal Inniskilling and 5th Royal Irish Fusiliers.

Alaunia : 6th and 7th Royal Dublin Fusiliers.

Canada : 6th Royal Irish Fusiliers.

Novian : 5th Royal Inniskilling Fusiliers.

One might be permitted to digress a little here. While at the Royal Barracks ten men of " D " Company were asked by Major Harrison, after he had been transferred to " A " Company on his return from sick leave, to go with him as N.C.O.'s for the latter company. It was a delicate question, this breaking away from the " Pals " in " D," but after a little talk they realized it was their duty to go. They received their reward when on the transport before the landing at Suvla Bay. The men who had transferred to " A " Company were thanked by the Colonel and the Major for what they had done, and it could be seen that what one might describe as an attachment had grown up between " The Old Toughs " * of " A " Company and the " D " men—although at first the latter had been jocularly called " The Young Toffs." Every one agrees that " A " Company were a fine lot of men. They were put on the first barge to go ashore at Suvla from the *Fauvette*; it was an " A " Company man who was the first of the 7th Royal Dublin Fusiliers to be killed, and they were always in the front line in the big fights.

* " *The Old Toughs* " *is the regimental nickname of the Royal Dublin Fusiliers.*

CHAPTER V

THE LANDING AT SUVLA BAY

ON the afternoon of August 5 orders were received that the troops should be ready to embark on Fleet sweepers for an unknown destination, and on the morning of August 6 the sweepers arrived—four altogether—and during the course of the day the troops were packed on them absolutely tight, with practically nothing but standing room. This applies specially to the two Dublin battalions. The 7th Royal Dublin Fusiliers were on the *Fauvette*. Each of the Fleet sweepers was in charge of a naval officer. The first left Port Hiero about twelve o'clock noon and the last about 4 p.m.

Strict orders were issued against smoking or noise on board, and every precaution was taken to make the ships as invisible as possible. No lights were allowed on board and no sailing lights were shown.

They steered a westerly course at first, so as to escape from the Turkish submarines and Turkish coastal observation, or the observation of Turkish spies, who were well organized on the Island of Mitylene and were supposed to have a wireless station in the interior of the island.

During the dark, early hours of the morning they came in sight of the Peninsula.

Cape Helles, which presented a wonderful sight, first appeared. Achi Baba was one mass of bursting shells. The morning was pitch-dark before dawn, and the sight was very fine. Some ships and the guns on land were engaged in a heavy bombardment. The bursting shells could be seen. Helles is about twenty-two miles from Suvla, and as they came up along the Peninsula, Suvla seemed about as far away as Wicklow Head is from Howth, and some of them thought the coast looked like Dublin Bay. The large naval shells bursting on Achi Baba suggested a house going on fire with a sudden blaze and immediately going out again, the noise sounding like one continuous roll of thunder. As they came opposite Anzac—about fourteen miles from Suvla—another bombardment was going on.

As dawn broke—just before five o'clock—they arrived in Suvla Bay. The morning was beautifully fine and the Bay was full of every kind of shipping, which was partly concealed by a low-lying mist. The naval guns were vigorously shelling the ridges round the Bay. The shells exploded with a bright red flame edged with a black fringe of smoke, just like a tulip with the red leaves tipped with black. The noise was terrifying.

The Fleet sweepers were ordered to anchor, and did so about a mile from the shore.

Day suddenly broke, and the sun as quickly rose, and as the light became stronger nothing was visible to the naked eye on the shore save the stretcher-bearers carrying wounded down the slopes of a hill, which the watchers were afterwards to know as Lala Baba. One could see a large number of men digging themselves in just behind the crest about half a mile from the shore.

The troops with General Hill immediately got orders to land, that is, the six battalions from Mitylene, including the 7th Dublins, and were to act under the orders of General Hammersley, commanding the Eleventh Division. About half an hour after they had anchored, shells began to fall round the Fleet sweepers. No ship was struck, but some of the shells burst very close. During the voyage from Mitylene, as indicating the spirit of the men, one could see various groups packed together as tightly as possible, playing the well-known Dublin game of " House "—which they continued until orders were given to land—even when the shells were bursting round the ship.

About 6 a.m. the lighters in which the men were to go ashore came alongside. Each lighter was capable of holding about three hundred men, and into them the companies were packed like herrings in a barrel. As quickly as possible they started for the shore.

The first two lighters reached the shore all right. The first barges were to land at what was known as " C " Beach, which consisted of pebbly white strand like that at Portmarnock, but not so wide, there being only about one hundred yards of strand inwards from the sea. The rest of the shore was like Dollymount—broken bits of sand and tufts of grass or wild thyme growing over small hummocks. This strand stretched from Nibrunesi Point in a south-westerly direction, for a distance of about four miles, to the rising ground at Anzac. Northward, the shore was rocky for about a mile, and then there was another beach, " A," which stretched round Suvla Bay to Cape Suvla, and about the middle was the entrance to Salt Lake. The landing was made practically at Nibrunesi Point, but at its south-eastern shore.

Behind the stretch of white sand, tufts of grass, and thyme, there rose a scrubby foreshore—sand with growth on it—about one hundred yards in depth, which brought us up against clay cliffs from twenty-five to fifty feet in height, rather like the shore at Killiney Bay. The cliffs were formed of shingle mixed with clay. They were not steep enough to give protection against shrapnel, but there were paths cut over them.

The first of the lighters to land contained one portion of the 5th Irish Fusiliers with General Hill and Staff, and one

61

portion of the 6th Inniskilling Fusiliers. They landed without any casualties, but just as they stepped on shore a heavy shrapnel fire was opened on the beach from four Turkish guns, which seemed to be situated on the rear slope of Chocolate Hill, and this caused a considerable number of casualties.

All through the landing of these battalions on " C " Beach on the morning of August 7 the Turkish guns alternated their fire on the beach and the lighters as they came in, usually four shells on the beach and then the next four on the lighters. One lot of the 7th Dublins, the first load, suffered most severely while in the lighters. Another lighter load, with another regiment on reaching the shore, was found to have had seventeen casualties, and the lighter itself presented the appearance of a shambles.

The beach at Nibrunesi Point was very favourable to landing, and the lighters were able to go right in, the dropping ends forming a gangway by which the troops got ashore dryshod. As each company reached the shore they were directed by a Staff officer left by General Hill for the purpose to take cover as far as such was available. First of all under the clay cliffs, and when these got congested to proceed inland under the slopes of Lala Baba. It was about two hundred yards from the clay cliffs to the sea.

Lala Baba rose in a gentle slope practically from the top of the cliffs. It had been taken during the night in a bayonet charge by two battalions of the Eleventh Division, and the evidences of that charge were only too apparent to the landing troops. Mutilated Turks and our own dead, some of whose clothes were burnt by the rifle bullets owing to the close nature of the fighting, lay about the slopes in every direction.

From the *Fauvette* the " Dublins " could see troops advancing in open order across the flat ground towards the hills. It was a splendid sight, and one that will remain

GALLIPOLI.

Scale of Miles

in the memory of " D " Company, being their first sight of warfare. They could see men fall as they got hit.

The 7th Dublins got ashore about the middle of the landing, proceeded to the rendezvous on the slopes of Lala Baba, and were more fortunate than those who remained at the strand. "A" Company went first, under Major Harrison, and " D " Company landed later, the lighter which took them ashore bringing back some wounded. Here they had their first sight of the horrors of war, the stretchers passing them with many of their burdens soaked in blood. The effect of this and of first coming under shell-fire when they landed was a severe trial, but they passed through it well.

As the morning progressed, the Turkish shells increased in number and high explosive was poured on the shore from about 9 o'clock as well as shrapnel. The high explosive caused casualties to the troops and was calculated to very much dishearten new men by the nature of the wounds inflicted, but all behaved splendidly and moved to their appointed stations and obeyed orders as if they were on review in Phœnix Park. No one ever thought of lying down until the order was given.

Unfortunately a field ambulance had established its headquarters at Nibrunesi Point, and, in addition, a signal company of the Engineers had set up a wireless installation there. The result of this was that many officers and men of the field ambulance and a large number of wounded were killed or mutilated by the Turkish fire. The Turks were in no way to blame for this, the real cause being the situation of a dressing-station in such a position where it was inevitably under fire.

As the morning went on five battalions were successfully landed on this beach. The remaining battalion, that is, the 5th Inniskilling Fusiliers, had to be diverted to " A " Beach, where General Sir Bryan T. Mahon, the Divisional

MITYLENE

VIEW OF MUDROS

WAITING UNDER LALA BABA FOR THE ADVANCE

THE 6TH MUNSTERS LANDING AT SUVLA POINT

General, landed with them, owing to the intensity of the Turkish fire on sea.

While the 7th Dublins were under Lala Baba they suffered no casualties, as the Turkish artillery confined its attention to the beach all the morning, with a few occasional shots at two mountain guns which were in position on the rear slope of Lala Baba, and were the only artillery on land at that time to support the advance of our troops. These two guns were a source of amusement to the men, as every time they were fired they ran backward down the hill with a sweating crowd of gunners chasing after them to haul them into position again.

CHAPTER VI

THE ATTACK ON CHOCOLATE HILL

THIS landing at Suvla Bay, in which "D" Company took part, was a portion of a larger strategic scheme of which a brief outline may be given, as it had been worked out carefully by the Commander-in-Chief of the Mediterranean Expeditionary Force, Sir Ian Hamilton. The unsuccessful struggles to dislodge the Turks, which had taken place in May and June in the southern end of the Peninsula and at Anzac, had indicated that large reinforcements would be necessary for carrying to a satisfactory conclusion the operations in this sphere of the war. Sir Ian Hamilton had determined that he could best employ these new troops which were available for him in a vigorous attack upon Anzac, combined with a surprise landing to the north, preferably at Suvla Bay, the object being to try to win through to Maidos, leaving behind a well-protected line of communications to Suvla. It was determined that this landing should be kept as secret as possible, and much ingenuity was exercised with success in misleading the Turks. Their only defences at that part of the coast were a girdle of trenches round Lala Baba and a few lengths of fire trenches round Hill 10. There was no barbed wire. Inland there were some guns on Chocolate Hill and Ismail Oglu Tepe, which could be brought into action against the Suvla Bay beaches.

The task set out for the 9th Army Corps under General Stopford, of which the Tenth Division formed part, was to seize and hold, immediately after landing, the Chocolate and Ismail Oglu Tepe Hills, as well as the high ground of the Kizlar Dagh range north and east of Suvla Bay. For this purpose the Eleventh Division had been landed on August 6 on the " A," " B," and " C " beaches of Suvla Bay. There is no doubt that the Turks were taken by surprise by this landing and were driven back from Lala Baba, as well as from Ghazi Baba, near Suvla Point, along the ridge of Karakol Dagh towards Kiretch Tepe Sirt, the two principal ridges of the Kizlar Dagh range.

The original intention had been that the Tenth Division should land at the Suvla Point end of the Bay, and by reinforcing the troops already attacking there drive the Turks farther back along the Kizlar Dagh range in the direction of Ejelmer Bay. In consequence of the inability of the Eleventh Division to dislodge the Turks from Chocolate Hill the original intention as to the Tenth Division had to be altered though not entirely abandoned. The 31st Brigade (less the 5th Inniskillings) and half of the 30th Brigade (6th and 7th Dublins) were landed at Nibrunesi Point, as we have seen, while the other half of the 30th Brigade (the 6th and 7th Munsters) along with the 5th Royal Irish Regiment (Pioneers) were landed at Suvla Point. As the rendezvous for the attack on Chocolate Hill was to be at the foot of Hill 10, the troops landed at Nibrunesi Point had to march there by Lala Baba under fire.

Sir Ian Hamilton has said in his dispatch dated December 11, 1915, page 33, that he had failed in his endeavours to get some live human detail of the fighting that followed at Suvla Bay. This and the following chapters are an effort to supply some of the information missing from his dispatch.

Shortly after landing it became apparent that Brigadier-General Hill had been ordered to use the five battalions under his command in support of an attack on the hills immediately south of the Salt Lake. A good view of the terrain was obtainable from the top of Lala Baba. At the foot of the land side of Lala Baba was a large stretch of sand which, at first appearance, seemed like one of those spots of shore on the western coast of Ireland which are flooded by the sea only at high tides. This was the now famous " Salt Lake." Lala Baba was connected to the north with the land by a narrow stretch of sand-dunes rather resembling those at Dollymount. It appeared that the officers, from the maps which had been distributed to them, had expected to find that the Salt Lake consisted of a sea of water with streams running into it, but there was no water of any kind, and the surface of the sand was covered with white patches which, on closer examination, were found to be deposits of crystallized salt—hence the name. Immediately on the land side of Salt Lake was a strip of ground covered with brushwood, out of which sprang the Chocolate Hill, about 150 feet high. This is what was seen looking due south from the top of Lala Baba.

Chocolate Hill has as an official name—Yilgin Burnu. There are several theories as to how it came to be christened " Chocolate Hill." Some say that it was the colour of the clay that was reached when digging the trenches ; others say that when the officers went to the top of Lala Baba to discuss their plans of attack, the hill was given its English name as an easy way of describing one of the leading features ; but the truth is that the Australian troops had it christened before the Tenth Division landed. The hill really was the colour of chocolate, the reason being that there was no herbaceous undergrowth or grass. The country was covered with scrub, below which was sandy earth. It had been burnt up by the gun-fire, and when the men came to see it closer it looked for all the world as if some one had planted shrubs in a hen-run. It was all scraped under the shrubs.

As our troops lay on the reverse slope of Lala Baba next the sea, terrific firing could be heard in all directions to their front, but no troops were visible there, so it was very hard to make out what was going on. They saw the two Munster battalions landing at "A" beach, and observed what they at first thought were shells exploding amongst them, but they afterwards discovered these were land mines. Very fortunately the Turks had not taken the precaution to mine any portion of Lala Baba. It seemed as if they had anticipated the landing at "C" beach, because trenches were dug right over the face of the clay cliffs. These trenches gave some welcome protection to those who had to remain there during the day. They seemed to be old trenches and had evidently been dug in the early part of the year when the Turks were arranging the defence of the Peninsula. Lala Baba itself had a considerable number of trenches towards its summit, and these were being improved by several battalions of the Eleventh Division, who were apparently in reserve. Farther along the beach to Suvla where there was an entry from the sea to the Salt Lake they could observe another brigade, or at least some battalions of the Eleventh Division digging themselves in.

On the northern slope of Lala Baba they saw burial-parties busy, and in every respect the general environment was not encouraging to troops who had never been previously under fire. Occasionally a shell burst over Lala Baba without doing any harm.

About 10.30 o'clock in the morning a message was received. They were told that the troops were being held up in an attack on Chocolate Hill and Sulajik, and that the battalions under General Hill were to reinforce them and press on at all costs. Immediately the advance was commenced by the 6th Inniskillings, two companies (" A " and " D ") of the 7th Dublins following, and on going round the bend on the northern side of Lala Baba, the troops came under a terrific fire of both high explosive and shrapnel, in consequence of which the advance was stopped, as it was obvious that very heavy casualties would be sustained.

About 11.30 a.m. as they saw that the Turkish fire had been diverted to the beach they immediately and successfully advanced across the narrow stretch of land north of Lala Baba. In doing so the battalions had to run the gauntlet of the Turkish guns. The 5th Royal Irish Fusiliers suffered very heavily, one shell bursting in the middle of one of their companies, killing and wounding a great number of men. However, the majority of the shells fell into the sea behind them.

After the first mile or mile and a half of the advance the men were ordered to remove their packs. This was done with mingled feelings of relief and regret, for the pack contained all that each man had except his rations, and when the pack was dropped he left behind a complete change of underclothing, washing materials, blanket and oil-sheet. It was said that these were subsequently collected near where they had been discarded, and ultimately most of the pile was burnt, through the kindly attentions of a Turkish shell.

It is creditable that the companies following in the rear of those that had suffered casualties, when they came to a scene of slaughter, simply opened out and passed on. It seemed to have no effect on the splendid spirit of the troops. Those who were killed in crossing the narrow strip at Salt Lake were merely buried where they lay. As the troops got across to the other side of the " neck " to the Salt Lake they extended their line in open order from right to left as follows :

(1) The 6th Inniskilling Fusiliers and the 6th Irish Fusiliers.

(2) Two companies of the 7th Dublins—" A " and " D."

(3) The 5th Irish Fusiliers ; while the remaining two companies of the 7th Dublins and the 6th Dublins formed the brigade reserve, remaining under cover of the sand-dunes immediately north of the neck.

The country was very open, there being practically no cover. Beyond the Salt Lake the ground, which rose at the shore, sloped down until at Asmak, which was a dry watercourse, it reached the level of the Salt Lake. The surface of it was about one foot higher than the sea. This ground afforded no cover whatever, but, strange to say, while the troops were crossing it no opposition was encountered. The Turkish guns during that period kept firing on " C " Beach and on the neck. The ground at the base of Hill 10 appeared to have been cultivated, but was merely earth with some slight growth of thyme and weeds on it. The smell of thyme pervaded the atmosphere all along from the shore to Chocolate Hill. While the forenoon had been excessively hot, there was a very heavy shower of rain about one o'clock which cooled the air a little.

They reached Asmak between two and three o'clock, and up to that point there had been no cover. Just as the firing-line reached this point, the Turks again opened fire, principally on the left of the 6th Inniskillings and on the two companies of the Dublins. The troops, however, advancing rapidly, crossed the watercourse, and on the other side reached good cover of brushwood, small hillocks, and rocks. Here the troops lay for some time, as the naval guns had opened fire on the Turkish guns, the position of which had been ascertained, and it was not until close on five o'clock that they effected an advance to the rising ground on the north of Chocolate Hill, when they came under a very heavy fire of shrapnel, and from machine-guns and rifles.

In that position they were about five or six hundred yards

from the bottom of the hill, where the Turkish trenches were situated in the scrub. It was apparent that Chocolate Hill was very strongly held, and as there seemed to be a net-work of trenches round the foot and on the crest of that position the troops dug themselves in.

While that was going on, Colonel Downing, with the remaining two companies of the Dublins, came up to the firing-line, having been in support until then, and they suffered some casualties as they came forward. This made two battalions at the foot of the hill within about six hundred yards, the 5th Irish Fusiliers being on the extreme left, the 7th Dublins being somewhat to the north side of Chocolate Hill and between that and the Salt Lake. For some time they remained in this position, as it possibly appeared unwise to advance under the circumstances with only the two complete battalions they had.

As we have previously indicated, the original plan had been for the Eleventh Division to land at Lala Baba and take Chocolate Hill and Ismail Oglu Tepe, which lies farther on towards Anafarta; while the Tenth Division, landed on the north of the Bay, were to take the Kiretch Tepe Sirt ridge of the Kizlar Dagh range. What actually happened was this:

The Eleventh Division by force of the Turkish opposition took a different direction and fought along the flat plain, thus allowing themselves to be enfiladed from the strong Turkish position on Chocolate Hill, which was completely surrounded by Turkish trenches, laid out very skilfully by the Germans. General Stopford, who was in command of the army corps, decided that Kiretch Tepe Sirt must take its chance with what troops he could spare from the Tenth Division, and that Chocolate Hill must be taken at all costs. He therefore sent off five battalions of the Tenth Division to take Chocolate Hill. These were two battalions each of the Dublins and

THE ATTACK ON CHOCOLATE HILL

Royal Irish Fusiliers with one of the Inniskillings. They took Chocolate Hill all right and got hold of the hill beyond, called Green Hill. There was then, of course, a big gap on their left, owing to the Eleventh Division having gone too far, and they were ordered to retire to Chocolate Hill and hold that.

The whole Division (Tenth) had been originally set aside to take the Kiretch Tepe ridge, but four regiments out of it, the Leinsters, Royal Irish Rifles, Connaughts, and the Hampshires had been sent the day before to get into touch with and reinforce the Australians, with the result that there were only eight battalions out of twelve available for the operations, and when the five battalions above-named—6th Inniskillings, 6th and 7th Dublins, and 5th and 6th Royal Irish Fusiliers—were sent off to take Chocolate Hill it left only the two battalions of the Munsters, the 5th Royal Irish Regiment (Pioneers), and the 5th Inniskillings for Kiretch Tepe Sirt to combat with the task originally assigned to twelve battalions. This explains why there were no reinforcements available either for Chocolate Hill or the Ridge, which were two of the strongest Turkish positions, and were undoubtedly taken and held mainly by the regiments of the Tenth (Irish) Division.

To come more to detail, about 6.30 p.m. our naval guns opened a heavy fire on the Turkish trenches on Chocolate Hill, and, as far as a spectator could judge, they appeared to almost blow the top off the hill. At the same time orders were issued that the hill must be taken before dark, and the 6th Royal Irish Fusiliers were sent up to reinforce, followed by two battalions of the 32nd Brigade.

The line for assault consisted of the 6th Inniskillings, 7th Dublins, and two companies of the 6th Royal Irish Fusiliers. Under heavy fire these battalions vacated the trenches they had dug and advanced in rapid rushes across the intervening ground. The rushes were by platoon after platoon. They had to cross ground which was very open and exposed to machine-gun and rifle fire from Chocolate Hill. It was uncultivated, with a few bushes here and there affording no substantial cover. The troops on the left, however, were able to advance over better ground, as it was much more closely covered with rocks and scrub, resembling the lower slopes of Ticknock.

They had come up beyond Asmak with the Lincolns and North Lancashires, who had been held up and were left under cover, and some of them came along with the Tenth Division in the attack. Between 4 and 5 p.m. Major Tippet was shot in the head while leading the advance of the 7th Dublins. The hill was captured a little before dusk in a general charge. Immediately before the charge four cruisers in the bay bombarded the hill for about twenty minutes. It made the top of the hill look like a volcano.

What has been said of "D" Company during that day's work?

"Under concentrated shell and rifle fire they took up formations almost as though they were on the Curragh. They had confidence in their leaders and they themselves retained coolness and courage, full of a determination to live well or die hard. They passed through infernos of shell-fire unshaken and even the thick rifle-fire from the Turks did not stop them as they charged the first ridge— Chocolate Hill."

Some time about 8.30 p.m. the 5th Royal Irish Fusiliers advanced round the north slope of the hill and captured the Green Hill, which was an under-feature of Chocolate Hill, and about six hundred yards farther off. Saturday night now settled down, and it was spent generally in consolidating the position and placing the troops, as well

Kavak Tepe

Anafarta Sagir.

Biyuk Anafarta

Scimitar Hill.

Green Hill

Burnt Hill.
Hetman Chair.

Hill

Country covered with low scrub.

Sulajik

Aznak

Ali Bey Chesme.

"Chocolate" Hill.
captured 7pm. 7th Aug.

Night March 12th Aug.

Salt Lake.

Hill 10

Opened fire for attack.

Kavak

Sand hills.

Beach B.

Beach A.

Beach C.

Lala Baba

Karakol Dagh.

Well.

SUVLA BAY.

Cruiser. shelling Enemy positions.
Cruiser.

Ghazi Baba

Transport "La Fauvette".

Suvla Point.

Nibrunesi Pt.

Landing 7th Aug. 1915.

British Trenches	——
Turkish "	– · –
Lines of March & Attack.	– · – →
Heights over Sea level in Metres.	50 ⌒ 100 ⌒
Scale of Yards.	0 1000 2000

as reorganizing the various units of the battalion. " D "
Company as well as " A " Company of the 7th Royal Dublin
Fusiliers held the main portion of the captured trenches
on the top of Chocolate Hill all the time.

As an illustration of the healthy rivalry between the
various companies and the keen spirit with which they
took up this fighting on August 7, the following extract
from a letter of an officer of another company, who had been
promoted from " D," will suffice :

". . . However, we pushed on without many casualties,
but I had lost touch with the rest of the company through
my connecting file being knocked out. However, I
joined up with another company of our battalion, whose
officer commanding told me to move on to Chocolate
Hill, about three miles distant, saying that Major Harrison
was in front of me, and telling me to connect up with
him, so I moved my platoon out in lines of sections with
ground scouts in front. Though I could not see any
sign of the rest of the company I pushed on till within
about one thousand yards of the hill, when we came
under rifle-fire, so I extended and took cover in the nearest
ditch. As the fire increased I decided to stay where
I was until I had a good look round with my glasses.
Through them I saw a number of the Turks leave their
trenches and come down into scrub on the slope of the hill,
so I opened fire, which immediately drew a heavy fire.
In a few minutes ' D ' Company came into our ditch with
a dash for all the world like a wild forward rush at Lansdowne Road. They were no sooner there than they were
away again. Their dash was fine and it freshened me up
no end. We were not long till we were upon them, as
we had been first up to this and had no desire to be pipped
on the post, especially by my old company."

THE ATTACK ON CHOCOLATE HILL

Another observer from the machine-gun section gives a vivid description of his experiences that day :

" It seems that by taking this particular route we upset the Turkish plan of resistance. You have seen the maps in the papers. They expected us to the right of Lala Baba and straight up on the right of the Salt Lake and close to the Anzac zone. They laid traps for us there, barbed wire and land mines, etc., which were cleared away by our engineers at leisure. To continue, we now took a half-right to Chocolate Hill, or Yilgin Dagh, and went across ploughed fields, fruit trees here and there and banks and hedges covered with beautiful flowers, which you would have given a lot for. All growing wild. About 2.30 p.m. Douglas sent me forward with the Colonel in case he had any message to send back from a position some distance ahead which he was going to reconnoitre. His own orderly, Grey, was with him. We chanced on a beautiful well and all refreshed ourselves and filled our bottles. Some troops were seen in front moving across to the right and the Colonel sent me to find out who they were, and a message if they were ours. Got across one field and then the bullets began to sing all round. I hid my rangefinder in a ditch and dodged the bullets for two fields more and finally got my message through. Some dodging on the way back. The bullets were probably not at me, but were coming over the heads of men I went to. Got my ' Barr and Stroud ' and returned.

" Soon we all had to shift from the well as bullets were too thick and troops coming up were drawing more fire. I went back to look for the section, but could not find them, hid behind tufts of grass, trees, and various other cover. Walked across fields and fields, but no one had seen them, and finally refused to go any farther until I

77

had something to eat. It was now dark and I felt safe to sit down. I met some 'B' Company, who put me on some 'D' Company in front, and there I had intended to remain for the night. These lads had no water and three of them collected all the bottles and I brought them along to the well. Going across a field I heard my name being called by our sergeant from a ditch, who recognized my voice. About half a dozen of the section were here with Douglas. I *was* glad to see them. The old Colonel was close by too, and he recognized me and said, 'Mr. Douglas will be glad to see you.' Well, we got the water and I joined up with the section and Colonel, and all moved off to get to our front line. We came to the bottom of Chocolate Hill and met a party coming down ('D' Company men), who told the Colonel the hill was ours and the Turks driven from the trenches. Great news for him. He was awfully bucked. I was requested to lead this party back to the well to get the bottles filled. I *was* tired, but off again. The well was surrounded by about two hundred thirsty Tommies fighting for the precious liquid. We got to the top of the hill again by one in the morning and then had to take up various positions. We managed to get a fine big dug-out for one gun emplacement, which had probably been used as headquarters by the Turks, there being straw on the floor and a seat cut. The excitement of the day was too great to allow me to sleep, so I went on guard until daybreak."

When landing, each man had had two day's rations with him, but when hunger affected them during the night it became evident that many of the troops had in the early part of the day thrown away their rations and emptied their water-bottles. It was a very fine night, but extremely dark ; there was no shelling, only occasional sniping. As far as possible the dead were collected and buried at the foot of Chocolate Hill. They are all buried in one place, and the 7th Dublins had a big casualty list of over one hundred, including Major Tippet and Lieutenant Julian. "D" Company lost twenty-two altogether.

The Turkish trenches which were taken were in the form of an oval encircling the top of the hill, with a communication trench running east in the direction of Green Hill and one west down towards the plain. They had not many sandbags in their trenches and had reinforced here and there with a

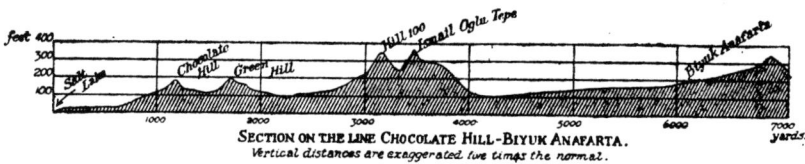

SECTION ON THE LINE CHOCOLATE HILL-BIYUK ANAFARTA.
Vertical distances are exaggerated five times the normal.

dead Turk. The greater diameter of the oval was about two hundred yards and the smaller diameter about one hundred and fifty yards. It ran round the entire top of the hill with numerous intersecting trenches. The eastward slope of Chocolate Hill was convex and the Turkish trenches, which were built in the form of a Grecian key, were badly sited, as there was a lot of " dead " ground between them and the foot of the hill.

The soil of the hill was a kind of hard brown earth mixed with shingle, but, notwithstanding this, the trenches had been greatly broken down by the continual firing from the naval guns, and in many places the parapets and trenches showed traces of only the most hurried repair.

A vivid description of his own experiences in the crossing of the sandy shore of the Salt Lake and of the subsequent attack on the hill was given a few days later by one of the company in a letter as follows :

79

" It was nearly impossible to walk or run in the soft, yielding sand. We went in single file across this spot close to the water's edge as it was a bit firmer. Then the shells started to pump their hail of death on us in proper form—high explosive and shrapnel—as fast as guns could fire. They had the range to a T.

" The sights I witnessed while going across there are just as well left out. I do not yet know how we managed to get over. The last twenty yards were by far the worst. The ground was soft, slimy mud, and then a sort of drain about four feet wide at the entrance to the lake. While crossing this a shell passed about six feet over my head and burst in this mud about fifteen yards to my left. I made a dive across the last gap and went up to my knees in the drain. Others were not so fortunate. They got mud up to the waist, but we were over and could lie down and get a ' breather.' After about ten minutes we got on the move again, and here I saw the first of the enemy lying dead.

" We had advanced too fast, and found our platoon was about half a mile ahead of the rest of the firing-line, so we hid behind a ditch until they came along. It was then about one o'clock, and I was feeling very empty and thirsty, while the heat from running was cruel. Had a few small biscuits and a mouthful of water, then on again by rushes from one cover to another, often a couple of hundred yards away, and across hard land just roughly ploughed. The going was terrible.

" I got to a ditch and had just taken cover when I got my first job of binding up a wounded man. He was hit in two places in the arm and the bone was broken. I got covered with blood when doing this, and it was about five days before I got the chance of washing the blood off again.

THE TOP OF CHOCOLATE HILL

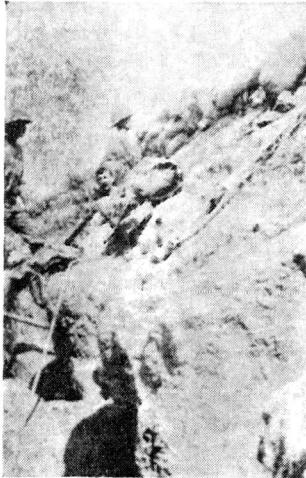

AN OUTPOST AT CHOCOLATE HILL

FROM TRENCHES ON CHOCOLATE HILL, LOOKING
TOWARDS THE RIDGE

"D" COMPANY IN TRENCHES, CHOCOLATE HILL
MOUNT, CLERY, LOOKER, D'ALTON,
F. BOYD, O'DONNELL

THE MUDROS CEMETERY

ADMINISTERING HOLY COMMUNION
CHOCOLATE HILL

" After I finished binding this man up a lot of our fellows had gone on, so I had to hurry to catch them up, as I did not want to get mixed up with other units.

" Young Keller and I were together and running for a ditch about eighty yards in front. We were pretty well ' puffed ' by the time we reached it, but found it crammed, so we had to take shelter at once. No looking round for a soft spot. This was all taken in when running up to the ditch.

" I spotted a small rise in the ground about three yards from the ditch. Quite a lot of fellows were lying out in the open to the left of this mound, and I was going to get down beside them when I saw I would be on the wrong side of this small scrap of cover, so I yelled to Keller, ' This way,' and flung myself down, with Keller a good second. The bullets hit the ground less than a yard away from my face, so, as I could not fire, I decided to keep down as much as possible.

" We were there about three minutes when the Turks got the range of us again, as we were on a sort of cart-track, and they potted the shells on it every time. I could feel the wind of the bullets from the shells pass over my legs, but my scrap of cover saved me. The place where the others were on the other side was riddled. I think Brooks was hit at that time in the body. He was not found until next day, and died very shortly after being taken to a hospital ship.

" ' On !' every time was the cry. ' That hill in front must be taken before dark ! ' I said to myself : ' Will this day never end ? ' The perspiration was streaming off us like water. Being five weeks without exercise had made us rather soft.

" We reached the foot of the hill at last, and got another decent bit of rest, and when we started to make our way up about 7 p.m. Major Harrison was leading us. He had a green handkerchief tied to a stick, waving it above his head. As he was nearing the trenches he collected his forces and found only about fifty of us. He sent word to those who were on the left and right that he was going to make the final charge at 7.50 p.m. This gave us about ten minutes' rest, so had a few hard biscuits and a mouthful of water. While waiting, the Turks turned a machine-gun on us, but the bullets all went high. Then a machine-gun from our side started at their trenches and the Navy sent a few shells at the hills, so we were in the midst of fire from three parts. We signalled to the Navy to cease firing as we were going to make a bayonet charge. Their shells landed quite close to us. Before making the final rush to the trenches we cheered for about a minute like madmen, and then the final rush—only to find one wounded Turk in sight.

" Then came the task of reorganizing and getting the different battalions and companies together. My word ! It was a job !

" A corporal called Tom Dale and myself got left in with ' B ' Company on the right side of the hill. We had to take our turn at sentry during the night. This meant going about ten yards outside the trench and listening for the slightest sound. By Jove ! it did try the nerves ! And the horrible smell of musk was sickening."

And so ended the first day of the Suvla Bay campaign !

CHAPTER VII

ON CHOCOLATE HILL

AUGUST 8–12

ON Sunday morning it seemed quite peaceful. There was hardly any shell-fire that day, save a few fired on the beach in the morning, and it was quite evident that at that point of time the Turks had been quite demoralized by our successful landing and advance.

A well had been discovered on the northern end of Chocolate Hill, but water could be obtained from it only in a very limited supply Another well was discovered on the western end of the hill, the water from which was, however, bad and muddy. Both wells were exposed to the fire of Turkish snipers, and this caused many casualties among men, parched with thirst, going to refill their water-bottles at great personal risk.

It was evident that these wells were totally insufficient to supply water for the troops on the hill, and the water-supply from the shore failed to arrive on Sunday morning, when the troops were all eagerly waiting for it, owing to the difficulties of transport—no receptacles being available. However, they had all their rations and such water as they wanted by three o'clock.

The 6th Dublins acted as the fatigue battalion, carrying up water, ammunition, and supplies to those in the trenches. These had to be carried from " C " Beach, via the seaward slope of Lala Baba and then over the Salt Lake, a distance of several miles and under an intense heat.

THE PALS AT SUVLA BAY

Near the trenches on August 8, the day after the Suvla landing, the thick scrub went on fire and the place grew so hot that they had to leave their portion of the trenches, afraid, at the same time, that the Turks might take the opportunity to make a counter-attack. Officers of other regiments round about gathered the men together to isolate the blaze and destroy it, but no one realized the importance of making some co-ordinate effort to put it out. Men were leaving the spot by the score, carrying their goods with them, when Major Harrison came along, and with characteristic promptness grasped the situation. He called on the men who were leaving the scene to lend a hand, and in a short time the fire was completely under control. His presence, as usual, had a most remarkable effect.

In the same portion of the trenches two men were making tea in their mess-tins over a little fire they had made, regardless of the fact that lots of Turkish rifles and ammunition had been captured about this position. As they were watching the tea brewing, some cartridges in the sand under their fire exploded, causing slight injuries to the tea-makers.

Some of the men found a considerable quantity of tea and sugar in the trenches, which they looked on as a veritable godsend, and rare good stuff they thought it. To show its value, we may say that when they marched out of the trenches on the Thursday night and Friday morning next, many of the men, already heavily loaded and wearied, carried the remains of the tea and sugar many miles through the long night march in pitch-darkness to the rest camp on the other side of the Bay.

During the day they buried all the dead Turks, some of whom had been found in the trenches, and the northern end of Chocolate Hill also caught fire. In this fire many Turkish dead were cremated, and traces were also seen of two German officers. After this fire they also suffered from the disadvantage of having the northern end of the hill perfectly bare, so that any man crossing it was exposed to the fire of the snipers. On the Sunday they also lost the support of two battalions of the Lincolns and the Borderers, who were withdrawn, leaving but the five battalions of the Tenth Division in the firing-line.

About the middle of the day a regiment arrived at Chocolate Hill, and were ordered to push forward to the famous " Hill 70," Scimitar Hill, which lay right between Chocolate Hill and the village of Anafarta, which was about sixteen hundred yards inland from Chocolate Hill. But when they got there they found that it was held by another regiment and they returned some time in the afternoon. It was afterwards stated that whatever regiment had been holding the hill withdrew on Sunday night after dark, and on Monday morning when daylight came this position was in possession of the Turks. As events afterwards proved, this was a very serious incident in the whole expedition, as the hill was held by the Turks throughout the whole subsequent operations on the Peninsula.

This hill, as well as " Green Hill," sometimes called " Burnt Hill " after the fire, which lay next in front of Chocolate Hill, and Ismail Oglu Tepe, was unsuccessfully attacked on August 8, 9, and 21. Heavy casualties were sustained by our troops in these attacks, all of which might have been avoided if the hill had been retained in our possession.

On Sunday night two companies of the 7th Dublins (" A " and " D ") formed the garrison of Chocolate Hill, and sent out a patrol which went from the front line almost into Anafarta village. The front line ran from about five hundred yards on the seaward side of Hetmanchair to Sulajik, two little houses dignified with the name of " village " on the map.

THE PALS AT SUVLA BAY

On Monday morning two battalions, the 6th Royal Irish Fusiliers and the 6th Royal Dublin Fusiliers, were attached to the 33rd Brigade under Brigadier-General Maxwell to attack the foot of the hills at Anafarta. One of these battalions had been withdrawn on the previous night to Chocolate Hill, and it was from there that the attack had to be made. Heavy casualties resulted in the advance over the open ground, and it was evident as soon as the attack had been launched that the Turks had been reinforced during the night, and the heavy machine-gun and rifle fire from the line of trenches, extending from Hetmanchair right across Green Hill, caused great slaughter. These had been occupied by them during the night. At the same time a heavy bombardment was opened by the Turks on Chocolate Hill, apparently with the intention of cutting up any reserves that might be lying behind it. Accordingly the troops on Chocolate Hill had to pack as tightly as they could into the trenches, and for many hours both shrapnel and high explosive rained on the hill. Sitting in the trenches, the sound of it seemed like that of a heavy storm, and the casualties were surprisingly small. Possibly the reason of the smallness of the casualties was that the Turks appeared to use nothing but field-guns, so that the trajectory of the shells was flat and consequently very few of the shrapnel bullets or shell splinters entered the trenches. Many shells of both guns failed to explode. Severe casualties were, however, caused amongst the troops at the foot of the hill and at the dressing-station which had been established there.

As far as could be judged the Turks seemed to have about three or four times the number of men in action that they had on the 7th.

It was a bright, fine morning when the attack started between six and seven o'clock. The attackers reached the foot of the hill and twice charged right up to the top, but were twice repulsed by the Turks with heavy casualties. During this time the battalion on the right ran out of ammunition, and "D" Company of the 7th Royal Dublin Fusiliers was called upon to supply them. Captain Tobin, with sixty men, was sent to bring up 20,000 rounds, and Captain Hickman, with eighty men, went for 40,000 rounds that were farther away. When Captain Tobin and his party got up they found the ammunition had been very urgently required and he and his men went farther up right into the firing-line with a portion of it. It was here that Sergeant Edward Millar was killed while gallantly assisting another unit to reorganize, for which he and Sergeant Burrowes received special mention in dispatches.

Captain Tobin gave his own account of it, as follows, in a letter to his father dated August 13 :

" On Monday I had my most trying experience so far. Our forces were attacking another hill, about six hundred yards from here, and of the same height, and had just got to the top when they were driven back. I had to take thirty-four boxes of ammunition up to the firing-line with sixty of ' D ' Company. This time I was out from 6 a.m. to 9 p.m. I got up into the firing-line under a hail of bullets and dumped along the ammunition, but not without losing six more of the company. When I got up we had to dig ourselves in under fire, as the enemy were in stronger numbers than we thought. As I was digging a bullet hit something in my bit of trench, and a bit of it hopped up and bruised me under the eye. After dark I managed to collect a few of the company and made my way back to Hill 50, where we are still entrenched."

This was his simple tale of what all who heard of it considered to be a most difficult and dangerous task. One often hears of the final assault of victorious and elated troops, but how seldom do the war correspondents let us realize the determined courage and steadiness required for a party, carrying with great labour the heavy boxes of ammunition, to progress slowly across open country right up to the firing-line in a burning sun, under deadly fire from the enemy.

The Turks had the superiority in number of machine-guns, which were well placed and did considerable damage ; and many of the machine-guns with the attacking battalions were soon put out of action by the Turkish batteries, though the Turks were heavily shelled by our Field Artillery battery from Lala Baba and by the two mountain guns from the scrub at the foot of Chocolate Hill.

In the afternoon, about three o'clock, the attack having failed twice, the whole of the attacking troops retired to their original line which had been occupied on the previous day, suffering many casualties in the withdrawal, the 6th Irish Fusiliers losing eight officers. The bombardment of Chocolate Hill had stopped about one o'clock, the Turkish fire being concentrated on the retiring troops. During this bombardment there was no water, the supply brought up the night before had been used up and the wells were under heavy fire, and no water was obtainable for the wounded, who were suffering greatly. About this time Brigadier-General Hill got out of the trenches, accompanied by Colonel Downing, and standing on the parapet with shrapnel bursting round them, called for volunteers to go down to the wells and bring up water. Every man in the vicinity immediately got out of the trenches, bringing all available water-bottles, and went to the well about three hundred yards away, accompanied by the General and Colonel Downing, filled the water-bottles and came back to the trenches again with a good supply for all who were in need of it, without suffering any casualties. Brigadier-General Hill stood on the parapet of the trench until every man had got into it safely, and after that the 7th Dublins would have done anything for him.

Nothing happened on Monday night, but on Tuesday morning, when the sun had well risen, the infantry of another Division, which afterwards proved to be the 53rd, were seen advancing across the Salt Lake under heavy fire, losing a considerable number of men. In time it was seen that their objective was Hill 70. They went straight at it, but by the time they reached the lines on Chocolate Hill they were considerably shaken from the casualties they had suffered. Their attack had artillery support from Chocolate Hill, one battery of the Royal Field Artillery (11th Division) having arrived there during the night. Chocolate Hill received a good number of shells on this day also, but nothing in the nature of a constant bombardment. The infantry pressed on past Chocolate Hill and up Hill 70, but for want of supports had to withdraw. A second attack, which was made about five o'clock, had the support of the troops of the Tenth Division, but it also failed, though the battery on Chocolate Hill maintained a heavy bombardment on the Turkish position.

One thing which was again evident from observation on Chocolate Hill on that occasion was the comparative immunity which the Turkish artillery enjoyed from the naval guns, which always proved so effective. There was no naval observer on Chocolate Hill, which was the only point of vantage, and messages sent back from the land forces locating the Turkish guns seemed to fail to reach the ships, or to be so long delayed as to be useless, owing to the Turks altering the position of their guns from time to time. A Turkish battery was located west of the village of Anafarta, but none of the naval shells reached it. However, the Field Battery on Chocolate Hill, which had been vigorously shelling this position, had destroyed an ammunition wagon, and for a considerable time the batteries ceased firing. This battery, unfortunately, had only shrapnel shell.

On Tuesday night the troops dug themselves in on the line they occupied, and General Hill, with the 31st Brigade, retired to " A " Beach. The 6th and 7th Dublins were left behind to garrison Chocolate Hill and Green Hill. The trenches on Chocolate Hill were deepened and improved, but the troops were considerably hampered in these operations by the manner in which the Turks had disposed of their dead, some being buried in machine-gun emplacements and a considerable number in the bottom of the trenches.

The engineer officer had advised the lowering of the parapet of the trench occupied by " D " Company, which was on the north-east and north-west corner of the hill, but when the attempt was made it was found that a good part of the parapet was composed of dead Turks, so the earth was only removed down to within a few inches of them—but the result was very unpleasant, and the smell became overpowering as the day got hot.

The machine-guns were placed in new emplacements, the one on the south side of the hill causing considerable inconvenience to the Turks at Hetmanchair when they left the trenches to draw water from a well, the position of which was conspicuously indicated when the sun shone on the new galvanized iron tank, which had been recently placed there by the Turks. The range of this was found very easily as a kind of road covered with dust went past the well and the strike of the bullets on it was very apparent. Every time the Turks appeared near the well the machine-gun was used with effect. It annoyed them so much that on Wednesday afternoon two Turkish guns opened fire on the hill with the intention of knocking out the machine-gun. They did not touch the gun, but caused a number of casualties among the field company of the Royal Engineers who were working at improvements in the trenches.

During all this period the face of the hill was harassed by Turkish snipers. One spot, near the machine-gun, which could not be deepened by reason of the rock, was a special mark for several of the Turks and some casualties were caused there, but ultimately a notice was put up : " Beware of Snipers." This notice caused considerable amusement and recreation to the men in watching the efforts of various persons to pass that corner of the trench on duty.

Wednesday and Thursday were also spent improving the trenches, and by the Royal Engineers in constructing a covered approach to the well on the west side of the hill. This well was also deepened by the engineers and a pump was procured from the beach, so that an ample supply of water was available without much risk. The engineers, however, lost a considerable number of men when providing for the safety of the infantry, four of them being killed by one shell. They worked and exposed themselves where necessary with great courage, and without the slighest hesitation, their good work ensuring the water-supply of the troops. They took the trench right down to the well, so that the men were able to go up and down under cover.

The wells at Suvla were very dangerous places. Snipers were always hidden within easy range, and the enemy's artillery had their position to an inch, so one could always see many dead and some wounded men round about them. The Turks even dropped a bomb on a well which had been newly discovered in front of the 7th Dublins and round which many men were gathered.

Here is an account of a day's work in the trenches from one of the Dublins :

" 4.45 A.M.—' Stand to arms ! Stand to arms ! ' I am half asleep and hear it echoed through the trenches, but

I still lie on, so up comes the sergeant : 'Come out of it, my lad. Stand to arms, stand to arms.' So out I get, grasp my rifle, with bayonet fixed, work the bolt, see that it is loaded, close it up again, and get into a firing position. At daybreak the order comes down : 'Unfix your bayonets and carry on as usual.' Then we all unfix, and all but the sentry sit down or carry on as they like, and the sentry remains on watch. The sentry is one man in every four at night and one in every eight during the day.

" 7 A.M.—'Come on there, here's this rum (strong language). Would you hurry up ? Do you want this . . . rum or not ? ' So shouts the sergeant-major, and we all gather round for a quarter-pint of neat rum, and it warms one, I can tell you.

" 7.30 A.M.—Breakfast. ' You cooked that bacon fairly well this morning, and these biscuits are all right.'

" Yes, they're not bad, and the tea's all right, not too bad for Gallipoli.' And so on.

" The meals are discussed, though not always with the same satisfaction.

" 8.30 A.M.—Rifle inspection. Usually means the sergeant making numerous rude remarks about the state of one's rifle, bayonet, etc.

" 9 TO 11.30 A.M.—Improvement of trenches, digging deeper, repairing parapets, making dug-outs more comfortable, etc., and of course all this time the sentries go on and come off as usual. Dong, Dong, Dong, Dong— four beats on the iron crowbar. A warning sound. Every one hears it, and in about two minutes we're all safe in our dug-outs. What's up now, you wonder. Well, it's an enemy aeroplane in sight, or else the enemy's artillery are going to shell our trenches. The Dongs are a signal from Headquarters, and then a few more casualties, some wounded, some killed—all part of the day's work.

Then people at home talk about ' Fight to a finish,' etc.,
while if they had a day of this they'd be peacemongers for
the rest of their lives.

" ' Dong, Dong,' two beats on the crowbar, and every one
is alive again.   The danger, whatever it was, has passed.

" 11.30 TO 1 P.M. is spare time, unless you chance to be on
guard ; then one o'clock dinner.   We usually make some
rice, then tea, and some biscuits and jam complete the meal,
while we have our bit of frozen meat and desiccated potatoes
in the cool of the evening.   It takes some cooking to do
those potatoes and leave them eatable, though if you get
them nicely done they're worth the trouble.

" 2.30 P.M. or so, and you're probably put on a sapping
party—that is, a trench which is being dug slowly in the
direction of the Turkish lines.   We dig out, say, a hundred
or more yards (this takes weeks), digging quite slowly,
and then we dig a new line of fire trenches and one night
we advance into them and the next morning the Turks
find us so much nearer to them.   I may as well say we do
all the advancing and the Turks do their best to hold us
in check, and although they don't always succeed they're
a pretty brave lot, and tough nuts to crack, also they fight
pretty fair and treat our wounded quite well, also any
prisoners they may take (they have very few).   I may
say they are, unfortunately for us, largely officered by
Germans, and very often think nothing of firing on a
Red Cross ambulance.   Indeed, I have seen them shell a
Red Cross wagon and follow it with shell after shell for
miles.   The first day I was here I saw a shell land straight
slap into the middle of a Base hospital.   It was an awful
sight, I can tell you, and terrible to see the poor wounded
fellows trying to crawl away to shelter, and the shells
coming down like rain.

" 5.30 P.M.—We have the promised late dinner, roast

beef (fried really), burnt biscuits, perhaps an onion, and some desiccated potato. With a little experience in cooking you can make quite a good meal.

"7.30 P.M.—' Stand to arms ! ' We repeat the morning's operations. The sentries are doubled, one in every four, which means that no man gets more than three hours' sleeep on end. Then one may be ' had ' for a listening patrol, a party that goes out about five hundred yards or less in front of the firing-line. Armed with rifle and ammunition you lie down and keep still, then if the Turks attack they meet that party first, who send back a message to our sentries and they wake up the rest and, meanwhile, the listening party endeavour to hold the Turks at bay as long as possible with rifle-fire, or bayonet if they come too close, retiring slowly till they come to the sap-head, where they jump in and rush for their lives back to the trenches, and God help the Turks who enter the sap-head after them, for it is always guarded inside with concealed bomb-throwers, whose deadly mines are about the worst things one comes in contact with.

"2.30 A.M. (perhaps).—' Stand to arms ! Stand to arms ! ' It is whispered rapidly down the line, you wake up and sleepily rub your eyes and inquire what's up. ' Turks attacking on the left flank and firing very hot in front,' is half shouted, half whispered at you. Meanwhile you can hardly hear for the noise of firing. You would imagine all the Turks in the world were firing, instead of perhaps a minor attack covering, say, a few hundred yards' front. After a while the fire dies down and all is still again, except for snipers' odd shots. The order comes : ' Unfix bayonets.' You unfix, and turn in again for a few more hours' sleep, and things go on."

The principal amusement of the men during this period

was endeavouring to locate the snipers and having shots at them.

The following incident is related :

"On the Wednesday morning (August 11) about twenty-five of us had to go over to the landing-place on a fatigue, and when going across the Salt Lake we had to look very 'nippy' because we were continually shelled. One was much safer in the trenches than out behind them. When we got to the Base we were not required, and as most of us had not had either a shave or wash for five days we decided to have a bathe, so we got into the sea just about the spot where we landed on the previous Saturday. Our dip was rather short, because a few shells came in our direction, and we had to clear out. Luckily we did, because we were no sooner out of the water when two shells landed right in the very place where we had been bathing. Our party returned safely with no casualties."

As they lay in the trenches they had a good opportunity of studying the nature of the land round about. The ground between Chocolate Hill and Green Hill was cultivated and the plots were separated by hedges. There were also trees and other marks of cultivation. At one spot in front of the trenches there were two corn-stacks, while on the other side the crop had just been cut and was lying in sheaves. In another place it was still growing. The fences consisted of small stunted oaks planted in rows along what is known in Ireland as a "sunk fence." It was in these small stunted oaks that the snipers hid themselves.

Lieutenant Drummond Fish, the well-known artist, who was with the Tenth Division in Suvla, has written of the scenery in the following graphic words :

"The colours were the most wonderful thing about Gallipoli. There were mornings when the hills were as rose as peaches—times when the sea looked like the tail of some gigantic peacock, and the sands looked like great carpets of glittering cloth of gold—the place was an inspiration in itself, and if beauty could have stopped a war, that scenery would have done it."

At twelve o'clock midnight on Thursday–Friday the Dublins were to be relieved from Chocolate Hill, but as the relief regiment came under fire on the way up it was 2 a.m. before the Dublins could leave the trenches and march back by Lala Baba to rejoin the Tenth Division, which was at Suvla Point, the extreme north-east corner of the Bay, where the "Rest Camp"—it proved to be a mere title of courtesy— was situated. From that day they operated as one of the battalions of the 30th Brigade. The route taken was first of all down the south-eastern slope of the Hill to the low ground south of Salt Lake, then across the south-eastern corner of the Lake, which was of course deep soft sand, to the landward side of Lala Baba, thence along the edge of the Lake to the narrow spit which they had crossed with such misgiving the previous Saturday prior to attacking Chocolate Hill, and from that point they skirted along "A" Beach to where the well was marked on the map at Suvla Point.

It was a wearisome, tiring, plodding march, through the darkness of the night to stumble along, every foot sinking deep in the soft clinging sand. It was not more than six miles, but it seemed sixty. Shortly before dawn the Colonel, who was always considerate of his men, resolved not to take them any farther until daylight, so they lay down where they stood and slept until dawn, when they moved on into the "Rest."

One man tells of the load he had on the long night march:

"I was given a box of ammunition to carry, also another rifle, so I had two rifles, my own 200 rounds, and this box of machine-gun ammunition. I struck after about half a mile, as I could not carry that load. They took the second rifle away, but left the box, and I had to carry that d—— box from Chocolate Hill, round Salt Lake, and right over to 'A' Beach. I never felt so done up in my life."

CHAPTER VIII

KIZLAR DAGH

KIZLAR DAGH is the name of a range of rocky hills running along the shore of the Gulf of Saros, half-way to Ejelmer Bay, having a steep slope almost from the top of the ridge down to the water's edge. Karakol Dagh is the name given to the lower portion of the range nearest to Suvla Point, while the ridge of Kiretch Tepe Sirt, the place with which this chapter is chiefly concerned, is the highest part of the range. It reaches its greatest height about three miles north of Suvla Point, where it is seven hundred feet above sea-level. It culminates in two peaks, one of which gives the name to the ridge, and the other was called by the troops " The Pimple."

The 7th Dublins had not had more than a couple of hours' sleep in the Rest Camp when between 6 a.m. and 7 a.m. they were awakened out of their heavy slumbers and ordered up, with the 6th Inniskillings and 5th Irish Fusiliers, to the extreme left flank of their own brigade on Karakol Dagh, where they were put in reserve to the 6th and 7th Munsters and the 6th Dublins, thus bringing together again the 30th Infantry Brigade, which had been split up since leaving England. Painfully, but with never a grumble, they struggle about a mile along the rise of the ridge, crossed over the summit and dug themselves in on the northern slope near the sea. One who saw them has written :

" I witnessed these regiments drag their weary limbs over the ridge of Karakol Dagh. The drawn face and haggard

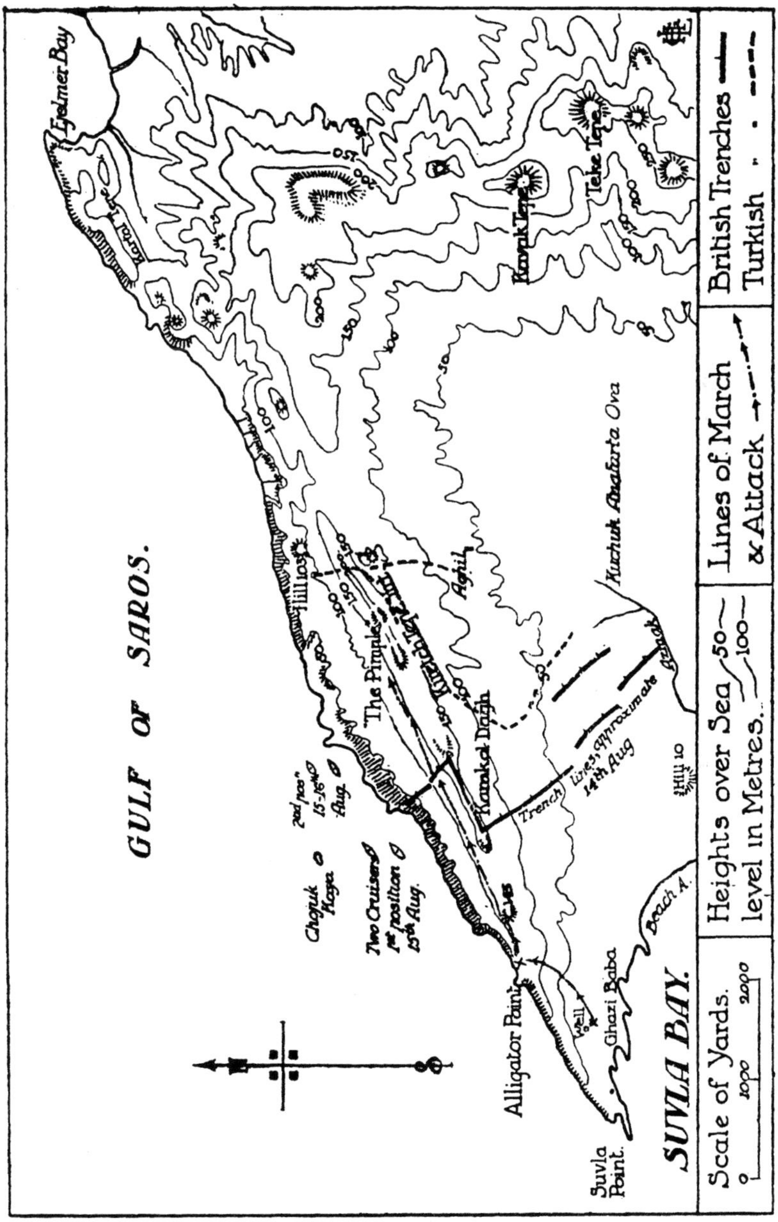
GULF OF SAROS.
SUVLA BAY.
Suvla Point.
Alligator Point
Ghazi Baba
Well
Beach A.
Two Cruisers 1st position 13th Aug.
Chojuk Kaya
2nd pos.n 15-16th Aug.
Hill 10
Trench
Lines, approximate 14th Aug
Karakol Dagh
The Pimple
Hill 105
Aghil
Kuchuk Anafarta Ova
Azmak
Kavak Tepe
Teke Tepe
Ejelmer Bay
Scale of Yards.
0 1000 2000
Heights over Sea level in Metres.
50
100
Lines of March & Attack
British Trenches
Turkish

look told of that dreadful week into which more privation and suffering had been compressed than fall to the lot of most men in a lifetime. Their faces were begrimed with smoke and sweat. The clay of the trenches showed on their hands and through the unshaven beard and close-cropped head, for water was still too scarce for washing purposes."

Here is a narrative of life in the reserve position on Friday and Saturday, August 13 and 14 :

" After we had moved up about two miles farther (from the Rest Camp), several men from our company had to go back to the Base for water. I was one of this crowd, and I remember getting the best feed I had for a few days when I got down there. I got some hot tea, biscuits, and jam. Oh, it was fine ! I also got one cigarette from a sergeant-major of the Royal Army Medical Corps. The first decent smoke for over a week. We carried up the water to where the battalion was, and when we arrived it was just getting dark, and the others, who had arrived some time before us, who were on fatigue, had just had a bathe, so we missed this treat.

" The following morning I was stuck for another fatigue—to go for picks and shovels to the Base—and while I was away the first mail arrived. It was the first news we got from home for six weeks, so, needless to say, every one was busy both reading and writing letters. Those who received ' fags ' were simply surrounded by fellows asking for one, because cigarettes were very scarce out there. I got six letters, so I was busy for the afternoon answering them.

" After having some more bully beef and biscuits at 6 p.m. we had a bathe, being only about one thousand yards from the sea at this place, and we could manage to get down for a dip. I was in such a hurry to get my grub down and off for the bathe that I broke some of my teeth, the biscuits were so hard. This was Saturday, August 14, and we were a week on the Peninsula. We had done a fair bit in that time, but there was worse to follow."

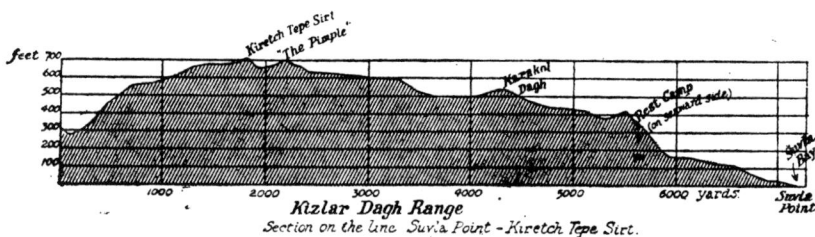

Kizlar Dagh Range
Section on the line Suvla Point - Kiretch Tepe Sirt.

During these two days (August 13 and 14), while the 7th Dublins were in reserve, there seemed to be heavy fighting going on in front, and an attack on the part of our troops was taking place over very difficult country, the enemy holding the farther hill—Kiretch Tepe Sirt—and the ground in front of it, which our troops were trying to take.

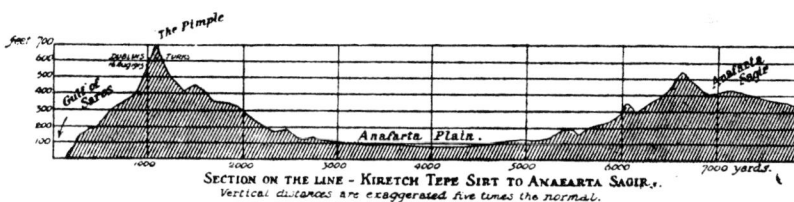

SECTION ON THE LINE - KIRETCH TEPE SIRT TO ANAFARTA SAGIR.
Vertical distances are exaggerated five times the normal.

The attack succeeded on the 14th, or early on Sunday the 15th; the Turks were driven well back towards the top of the ridge and some prisoners were taken, but the attackers suffered very heavy casualties.

Though the position which the 7th Dublins held while in reserve until the forenoon of Sunday, August 15, was sufficiently near the sea to enable them occasionally to have a bathe, they were under shrapnel and rifle fire most of the time, and the dug-outs and other cover seemed hardly sufficient for their protection.

The various Church services had been arranged for the forenoon of Sunday and were held shortly before orders were given for a general advance along the ridge.

From where the front line of the 5th Inniskillings, 6th and 7th Munsters, and 6th Dublins was on Karakol Ridge the ground to the north-east was gradually rising to the top of " The Pimple " on Kiretch Tepe Sirt, eight or nine hundred yards ahead. The objective of the troops was to secure the ridge line of Kiretch Tepe Sirt and the ground straight ahead, between the ridge and the sea as far as Hill 103.

First of all the torpedo-boats down below shelled the top of the hill, driving the Turks to cover. Then the regiments named went ahead in the first line. Along they went in short rushes, and, finally, when they had almost reached the top of " The Pimple," they fixed bayonets and charged in one mass right over the ridge. Every one started cheering, as if they heard the cheer of the attackers ; even the sailors on the gunboat below sent up a tremendous cheer, and the troops in reserve yelled themselves hoarse. The charge was a complete success, as the Turks were dislodged and a considerable number of prisoners taken. They were all fine fellows physically, and seemed quite contented and pleased with their fate.

On that Sunday afternoon about three o'clock the 7th Dublins were ordered to get ready to advance to the firing-line and reinforce the 6th Dublins and the 7th Munsters, who had suffered heavy casualties, and to hold the hill. Later in the afternoon they moved off and found that the fighting that was proceeding was of a terrific nature, the Turks keeping up a persistent and deadly fire with machine-guns, shrapnel, and bombs.

KIZLAR DAGH

It was when the 7th Dublins were about half-way up between Karakol Dagh and the top of the ridge that Colonel Downing was severely wounded in the foot by a sniper who had taken three shots at him, getting him at the third. It was found to be so serious that he had to be removed to hospital—a great loss at a time when

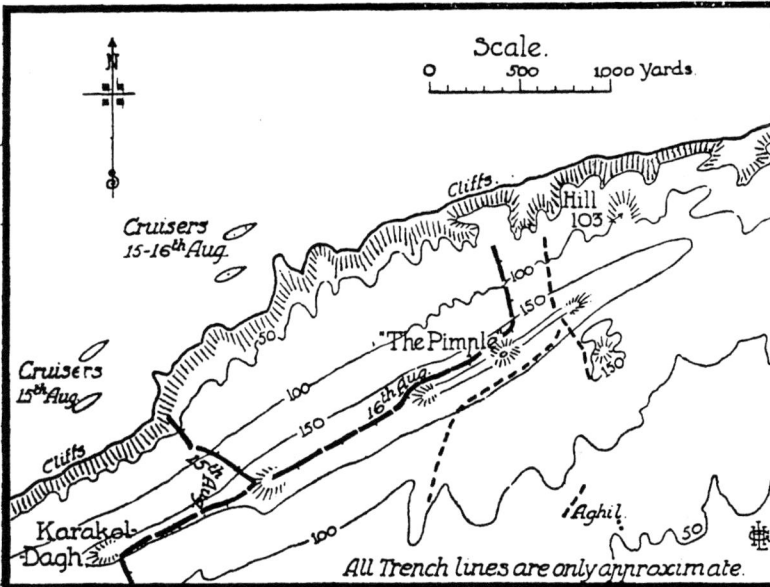

sound judgment, courage, and cheerfulness were most required.

About eight o'clock the 7th Dublins took over the position at the southern end of the ridge, and at this time the Turks still held some trenches in the direct front near the top of the hill on the sea side of the crest, but were in much greater strength on the inland side of the ridge. "B" Company of the 7th Dublins had been sent under Captain Leschalles to dig in from the top of the crest down towards the sea so as to hold the enemy in the direction of Hill 103. Near to the northern end of the ridge this line from the sea turned at right angles and ran parallel to the coast, slightly below the crest, for nearly half a mile, along which it was held by the 5th Irish Fusiliers and 6th Munsters to some distance past "The Pimple," on which was a large knoll or cairn of stones about fifteen or twenty feet square and composed of large boulders. It was of peculiar formation, like a huge basin of stone, surrounded by rocks. The rest of the line then turned back towards the southern end of the ridge and was held by "D," "A," and "C" Companies of the 7th Dublins in that order. "D" Company held about three hundred yards of the front nearest "The Pimple." Then came "A" Company under Major Harrison and Captain Fitzgibbon, and at the extreme right facing the valley was "C" Company under Captain Palmer. The 7th Dublins held on splendidly, but unfortunately suffered many casualties, and soon after 10 p.m. the Turks, strongly reinforced, made a fierce counter-attack upon the hill, during which the rain of bullets and the fire of the machine-guns was the worst the Dublins had experienced since their arrival on the Peninsula. They were, however, able to hold the enemy in check, their rifle and machine-gun fire mowing the Turks down in dozens and driving them back to the foot of the hill. Fearing a return visit of the enemy, listening-posts from all the companies were sent out that night between the line of the ridge and the Turks. "D" Company's post were mostly from No. 16 Platoon.

Sure enough, just before dawn, about 2 a.m., the Turks in still greater force made another attack, and the covering party had only time to give warning to man the ridge when the enemy again attacked the hill with great fierceness, and tried to retake it. The Turks had sent out a large party of bombers with hand-bombs in front, backed up by machine-guns and infantry on the flank. The bombers took up a strongly protected position on the other side of the ridge

THE RIDGE

ON THE WAY TO "THE PIMPLE"

IN THE TRENCHES, KARAKOL DAGH

THE REST CAMP

SERVICE IN A GULLY

THE CEMETERY, CHOCOLATE HILL

from the Dublins, with the machine-guns and infantry to cover them from the right flank.

The position then was this. There was the rugged knife-edged ridge six hundred feet above the sea, which ran from north-east to north-west parallel to the coast-line, and about eight hundred yards from it. It was covered with thick, almost impenetrable, prickly shrubs and undergrowth and large boulders, which made progress very slow and difficult. The top was covered with boulders, which in many places were standing up on end like huge slabs—a natural barrier. The ridge sloped sharply to the sea on the side which was held by the Tenth Division, while in the direction of the advance over the ridge it went sharply down a steep gully, almost precipitous at first. On the sea side right at the top were the so-called trenches of the 7th Dublins, merely barriers of rock, and about ten yards on the inland side of the ridge the Turkish bombers had got cover under the shelter of the overhanging rocks and in great strength just below the large knoll. This was on " The Pimple " and higher than the surrounding ground. A few could get on this knoll for observation or the like, but it broke up some-what the contour of the ridge so as to prevent a general move at that point over the crest.

The Turks remained in their position under the shelter of the crest and " lobbed " the bombs over the ridge among the Dublins, causing terrible casualties. The Dublins had no bombs and when they endeavoured to retaliate they had to creep, two or three men at a time, to the crest and, leaning over, fire downwards at the concealed Turks, or roll large boulders down on them, thus necessarily exposing themselves. It was enough to dishearten and try the bravest and most experienced troops to be in such a helpless plight. But they held on to the position for several hours, being practically unable to do anything by way of defence except " sit tight " and trust to luck. Then shortly after six o'clock, in the bright early sunshine of the morning, came the incident which, to the 7th Dublins and especially "D" Company, was the most fateful of the campaign. Somewhat earlier in the morning, before dawn, "C" Company under Captain Palmer had been taken to reinforce the firing-line at the left, where it was being sorely pressed near the knoll. This was the hottest corner of all, and twice the line wavered and nearly broke, but with grim determination still held on. Major Harrison, who had until then been with "A" Company on the right of the line, sent word for as many of "D" Company as could be spared from the portion of the line that they held to be sent to further reinforce the left, and when they came he told them the only chance of keeping the hill was to charge the bombers. To every one it was obviously a deadly undertaking, but no one flinched. Those who were first to get out, mostly from No. 14 Platoon, fixed their bayonets and, having had indicated to them the position of the bombers, with a terrific shout rushed off to the top of the crest, led by Captain Hickman, some going through a huge gap that had been made at the side of "The Pimple" by the naval guns shelling the ridge the previous days. Immediately on coming into the open a bullet struck Captain Hickman and mortally wounded him.

The men never stopped, but Major Harrison, without a cap, and waving his cane, rushed forward, and calling out, "I will lead you, men," dashed out in front. He got as far as the edge of the Turkish trench, which was about ten yards in front, when he was struck in the body by a bomb and killed. Almost every one in the charge was killed or wounded by the machine-gun fire from the right flank; and only four, Sergeant Burrowes, Sergeant Drummond, and Privates Synnott and Verdon were able to crawl

106

back over the ridge to the cover from which they had come. Captain Tobin was now left as senior commanding officer of the company, and after the disastrous results of the charge he went among his men encouraging and steadying them; then he made his way to the knoll where Lieutenant Hamilton already was, to see exactly the position of the Turks and decide what should be done. While there, he received a bullet in the head which killed him instantly.

As the effort to dislodge the bombers by bayonet charge seemed hopeless, Lieutenant Hamilton, now left in command of the company with Sergeant-Major Kee, afterwards mentioned in dispatches for distinguished gallantry, decided to remain on the defensive until reinforced or relieved. The bombing of the Turks still continued with great ferocity amid shouts of " Allah! Allah! " and some of the Dublins were seen at times actually catching the bombs as if they were cricket balls and throwing them back. Private Wilkin was specially mentioned in dispatches for heroic conduct at this period. He caught in succession five bombs and hurled them back, but as he caught a sixth it burst in his hand and blew him to pieces. By his gallant and self-sacrificing conduct he saved many of his comrades. One could hear the wounded calling out in front, but nothing could be done to assist them, and rescue was quite impossible. Further charges would have been a useless sacrifice of life, and might have led to the loss of the position. In spite of the hail of bullets that any exposure drew, the men continued steadily firing. Round about among our men lay the dead and dying, the latter parched and suffering, but not a drop of water to be had for them until hours had elapsed.

About nine o'clock the 6th Dublins and two companies of the 5th Royal Irish Regiment (Pioneers) arrived to relieve the firing-line, and about 9.30 p.m. the 7th Dublins withdrew about a mile, where they got some water, and as they moved farther down, some tea—a welcome draught.

It was during the struggle on this ridge in the early hours of the Monday morning that Lieutenant Weatherill, one of the original " Pals," was killed. His company commander, Captain Leschalles, and Lieutenant Russell of " B " Company also fell. On the Sunday afternoon Lieutenant Weatherill had gone with " B " Company and the engineers to make the trench from the top of the ridge down toward the sea and occupy it. In carrying out this order in the dark his platoon got out of touch with the remainder of the company, and he accordingly ordered them under cover and went out himself to find his whereabouts. He went up to the top of the ridge where another regiment was keeping the right flank. He found they had lost all their officers except one young subaltern, who was wounded, and all their non-commissioned officers save a lance-corporal. He came back for his sergeant, and with the help of the men on the ridge they got the position consolidated. Thinking it his duty to stand by the other regiment during the night he sent the sergeant back. On the Monday morning when the sergeant heard the heavy fighting on the ridge he sent up for news of Lieutenant Weatherill, and was told he had been killed at daybreak. Lieutenant Crichton, who had also become aware of the plight of this regiment, during the night had gone up with Sergeant A. Crookshank to assist them. Both of these were also killed in the counter-attack. This readiness to take responsibility, act in emergencies on their own judgment, and help others regardless of personal safety was characteristic of " D " Company men throughout the whole campaign. There were many instances of which the foregoing are merely examples.

Of the Sunday night before the counter-attack of the

dislodged Turks and the days following, one of " D " Company, with great vividness, writes :

"We were in reserve to the 6th Dublins and 6th and 7th Munsters. They took the hill called ' The Pimple '— nothing but big stones and short scrub. It was taken about six in the evening. We took it over from them about 8.30 o'clock.

"During the day we had been under cover about a mile back, from about eleven o'clock that morning. Then the fun started. We could see the Turks quite easily.

" Jack Boyd and I were lying together keeping watch, and about 11 p.m. I said : ' What about something to eat,' as we had had only a bit of ' B.B.' and a few biscuits since morning, and our bare quart of water, which was half gone by this time. We divided a tin of bully beef, and had a good supper and nearly finished our water. The last meal poor Jack ever had.

" By morning our bottles were empty, and no prospect of getting any more. At 3.30 a.m. their counter-attack started.

" Brown from Clontarf was opposite me, as well as J. B. He got a graze on the left temple. The bullets knocked dirt into my face. By Jove! It was a hot time then! Their bombs started. Such a row! It was just like a living Hell, and I have no clear remembrance of anything!

" Next item was our bayonet charge, headed by Hickman. He was killed, Jack Boyd and Willie Boyd and young Keller also, and some others. Lex was wounded and Drummond. I was one of the last out, and when about twelve yards out could not see any of our fellows except *one*, who, as I thought, lay down, so I lay down as well. I looked around, but could not see any one to support, so I said : ' Here's a how-d'you-do. If I stay I will either get killed or wounded. If I get wounded I will lie here all day, and I have no water in my bottle, so I had better make a dash for our lines, and if I get shot—well, it cannot be helped, but I have the chance of getting in.' While debating this over in my mind I was lying quite close to a chum called Cecil Murray (from the Bank of Ireland); he was badly hit. I asked him where he was hit. He showed me his left hand, which was in pulp, and, while speaking to him, he was hit three times in the body. The groans were heartrending. Then a young chap called Elliott, who played ' footer,' was shot in front of me when running out; he jumped about three feet when hit; he started trying to crawl back to our lines, and just got above me when he was hit again. He died in a few minutes. Then came my dash for safety. I made two rushes of it, and had to shout to our fellows to stop firing to allow me to get in. I got a splinter of a bullet in the side. It just pricked the skin and stuck in my belt. There is a hole in my belt where it stuck. When I got behind the line, the first thing I saw was Lex, bandaged all over the head and shoulder, but could see no one else there. There were no stretcher-bearers of any sort, so I got permission from Lieutenant Hamilton to help him down the ridge. I then discovered my knee was cut and swollen. Either another splinter of a bullet or cut by the rocks. I could hardly walk. The sights I saw going along that place I shall never forget. Some of our fellows throwing back the bombs which the Turks threw over and which had not exploded. One fellow caught them like catching a cricket ball. Wounded and dead lying everywhere. The sun streaming down and not a drop of water to be had. Neither had we bombs to reply to the Turks and drive them out.

" We were relieved about 8 o'clock and then went back

to our dug-outs about one mile back. Just as we were getting our dinner, two shells came along, and one fellow from 'A' Company got his head blown off, and Sergeant Kenny of 'A' Company, an 'Old Tough' of the 2nd Royal Dublin Fusiliers, lost a leg. Our only officer left was Hamilton, badly wounded in the foot. Our platoon numbered about sixteen, and three of us were left of No. 8 Section—Hanna, Egan, and myself. It was a miserable time. That night we went up again, but not so far as in the morning. We had retired about half a mile."

The torpedo-boat destroyer lying about eight hundred yards away on the left flank, in the bay, had been very precise in firing her shells, otherwise many of our own troops would have been killed instead of the Turks, and when night fell she turned her searchlights on the scene and still shelled the Turks with their aid.

Many of the wounded came through terrible experiences, such as the following :

" The platoon was rushed into that deadly corner on the ridge overlooking the Gulf of Saros about an hour before daylight. The place was already a shambles and we could almost shake hands with the Turks, who were behind the low stone earthwork armed with bombs.

" I remember how sore my shoulder had become with firing, when three bombs, one after the other, fell four feet away among the stones on the steep slope of the ridge. After scrambling to reach the third as it rolled, I received a blow in the chest from the explosion which made me helpless for about eight hours. I remember the 7th Dublins being relieved, but could not follow, and saw our dead and wounded in the grass and scrub fire that took place subsequently. Failing to get more than a few yards towards safety, I decided to lie in the scrub all night and at dawn to make good my escape. I had no water, as my water-bottle had been smashed by a bomb.

"Next morning, after much trouble and excitement avoiding hidden snipers, whose bullets often whizzed unpleasantly close, I found water, and then safety, by getting down the cliff to the beach—travelling along the latter waist-deep in water sometimes, and then swimming round the headland, where the Navy were very busy pumping fresh water ashore."

CHAPTER IX

FROM KIZLAR DAGH UNTIL THE WITHDRAWAL

ABOUT 10 a.m. on the Monday morning (August 16) the battalion was taken from Kizlar Dagh and marched back to their dug-outs on Karakol Dagh, a sad and downhearted crowd, with many familiar faces absent. Lieutenant Hamilton, the only officer left in " D " Company, though wounded in the foot, was in command. It was a sad roll-call for the regiment. Their casualties during the night stood at 11 officers and 54 men, killed or wounded, and 13 missing; " D " Company, which had landed 239 strong, being now reduced to 108 all told.

After some rest they were taken back in the evening to their old position on the ridge, which they held until the general evacuation of the position the following Tuesday (August 17). " D " Company came back on Tuesday night as a fatigue party and moved all the battalion stores, etc., from the reserve position down to the shore near Suvla Point, where the other three companies joined them. On Wednesday (August 18) they were moved round the shore to a more sheltered gully, where there would be more protection from shell-fire. They were kept occupied making roads for the mules among the hills and down towards the sea-shore. The original line held on Karakol Dagh from which the advance was made on the previous Saturday was now taken over by some Territorials.

The official dispatch has a very vague and scanty reference to the battle, having regard to the appalling casualties and the heroic character of the fighting. The following is the ex.ract: " The 30th and 31st Infantry Brigades of the Tenth (Irish) Division were to attack frontally along the whole ridge. . . . After several hours of indecisive artillery and musketry fighting, the 6th Royal Dublin Fusiliers charged forward with loud cheers and captured the whole ridge together with eighteen prisoners. The vigorous support rendered by the naval guns was a feature of this operation. Unfortunately the point of the ridge was hard to hold, and means for maintaining the forward trenches had not been well thought out. Casualties had been very heavy, the 5th Royal Irish Fusiliers having only one officer left, and the 5th Inniskilling Fusiliers also losing heavily in officers. Reinforcements were promised, but before they could arrive the officer left in command decided to evacuate the front trenches. The strength of the Turks opposed to us was steadily rising and had now reached twenty thousand."

Shortly after this Brigadier-General Nichol sent the following message to the 6th and 7th Dublins and 6th and 7th Munsters : " Brigadier commanding wishes to express his thanks and admiration to all ranks for their conduct during the trying operations since landing on the 7th inst. They have cheerfully undergone the greatest of all privations from the want of water, and their conduct before the enemy has been beyond all praise. Few troops have been called upon to undergo a more severe trial than they did between the evening of the 15th inst. and the evening of the 16th inst. The Brigadier deeply regrets the terrible losses the Brigade has sustained."

The Turks during the remainder of the campaign were never dislodged from Kiretch Tepe Sirt. They fortified it with five lines of trenches, and subsequently when the Dublins were in trenches or reserve at the north side of Chocolate Hill, looking across the plain to the Turkish position on the rear slope of the hill they could see the Turks moving about between the trenches and still pursuing until the last their consolidation of the position. The Turks also succeeded in placing some heavy artillery near " The Pimple," which gave a good account of itself later, much to the discomfort of our troops.

The attacks on the Kizlar Dagh range during the preceding three or four days had, as we have said, caused many casualties among the officers in the regiments of the Tenth Division engaged in these operations. In consequence of this it became very necessary to fill their places, and there was little inclination at such a critical time to bring out untried men from England, even if time had permitted of it. Accordingly on August 19, by the order of General Sir B. Mahon, the " D " Company was paraded to obtain volunteers, from whom a sufficient number of officers might be selected. Many of the men preferred to stay in the ranks with the " Pals " and continue to fight together as privates. However, as a result of this, the following were gazetted as Second Lieutenants, dating from September 14, 1915, when their selection was confirmed by the War Office : Corporal A. M. Ewen, Lance-Corporal W. J. Mount, Corporal D. M. Frazer, Corporal W. H. Sargaison, Sergeant J. R. Clarke, Private J. Bull, Private J. W. Roberts, Private A. P. Hunter, Private J. F. Cox, Lance-Corporal W. R. McFerran, Lance-Corporal E. H. Verdon, Private A. Dalton, Sergeant G. Hare, Company-Sergeant-Major Wm. Kee, Sergeant S. Kaye Parry, Sergeant A. E. Burrowes, Sergeant A. H. Murray, and Private T. O'B. Hickman. The last six names received their commissions in their old battalion. After this " D " Company seemed to lose its identity, so many of the old faces were gone.

From this period very little detailed information is forthcoming as to their movements. At midnight on the 20th they were marched back to a point beneath the cliffs of

THE PALS AT SUVLA BAY

Lala Baba, about a quarter of a mile south of the spit of sand over which they had crossed after the landing of August 7. This change of position was preparatory to taking part in the great consolidated attack which had been arranged for August 21. It appears that after the failure of the operations immediately subsequent to the Suvla landing General Birdwood had hoped to make a fresh attack on Sari Bair provided he might reckon on a corresponding vigorous advance being made by the new divisions in the Suvla Bay district on the important hill Ismail Oglu Tepe. This could not be carried out at once, and the interval had been occupied by General Stopford in strengthening his line, which ran from the Kizlar Dagh through Chocolate Hill, and it was for this purpose that the operations of August 15 and 16 had been carried out by the Tenth Division, the object being to straighten out the left of the line by gaining possession of the crest of Kiretch Tepe Sirt.

The special objective of the battle of August 21 was the steep hill Ismail Oglu Tepe, which forms the south-west corner of the Anafarta Sagir spur. It is the strong natural barrier against any invader from the Ægean Sea marching against the Anafartas, as the British troops were doing. The hill rises 350 feet from the plain, and being covered with a dense holly-oak scrub is almost impenetrable, as the troops have to move in single file along narrow goat-tracks through the bushes. Another great difficulty was the open nature of the only ground available for the concentration for attack. The only cover was Lala Baba and Chocolate Hill, the remainder of the ground being an exposed plain.

The scheme of the attack was that while two Divisions held the Turks from Sulajik to Kiretch Tepe Sirt, the Twenty-ninth and the Eleventh Divisions would storm Ismail Oglu Tepe, the Tenth Division being in reserve along with the Second Mounted Division. This scheme is said by Sir Ian Hamilton to have failed principally for the reason that by some freak of nature Suvla Bay and the plain were wrapped in a strange mist which rendered an accurate bombardment of the Turkish position from land or sea a very difficult task. Hence the heroic attacks of the infantry on the Turkish position were unavailing. The losses fell most heavily on the Twenty-ninth Division. They were just under five thousand. This was the last of the big attacks made on the Peninsula.

To return to our narrative of the 7th Dublins. They stopped at Lala Baba until the morning of Saturday (21st), when they were told that the naval guns and artillery would bombard the Turkish positions towards Hetmanchair from 2 p.m. until 4 p.m. They were to be in support of the attack, which was to be launched by the Eleventh Division at 4 p.m., when it was expected that the sun being against the Turkish position would show up their trenches in the strong light. The 7th Dublins were to extend southward from Chocolate Hill towards Anzac on the rising ground inland from " B " Beach to Nibrunesi Point. They moved out over the open ground to the south of Lala Baba in the direction of Hetman-chair, companies in order A, B, C, and D, and when they had advanced about half a mile they formed into extended order, " D " Company being on the southern side of the stream Asmak Dere, to occupy the trenches which had been evacuated by the Division which was attacking. As the attack was unsuccessful by reason of the Turks being in great force, and in practically impregnable positions, the attacking Division had to withdraw again to its trenches, with the result that the Dublins spent most of their time moving in the open from one trench to another under very heavy shell-fire, suffering many casualties.

A description of the early portion of this battle has been vividly given as follows :

THE PALS AT SUVLA BAY

" By the way, the first really big action I was in was the attempted advance on the 21st. I expect that you saw about it. We were acting as reserves and had to advance about two miles under terribly heavy shell-fire, mostly high explosive, thank goodness! I say that because shrapnel is miles away the worst as regards troops, though, of course, in a bombardment the most valuable is the high explosive. The shells were bursting at about the rate of twenty per minute (as I've heard it said), which means there was practically never a second that one was not exploding. We advanced in long lines, single file of course, and so on right across the front. The shells, thank God, mostly seemed to drop in the gaps. Then, as we got clear, we changed our formation and advanced in practically single file with a yard or more between each man, and here again we had wonderful luck, for all the shells seemed to burst either in front or just behind that line, of course many dropped right on it, and the casualties were heavy enough, but not half what they might have been. I really don't know how I ever reached the trenches. I was fully expecting to be blown to eternity every minute. It was about the nearest approach to the mythical Hell that one could imagine; the whole place was in flames, as was also a large tract behind the Turkish lines. However, here I am safe and sound, and feeling not a bit the worse."

It was about this time that the company felt most the loss of so many gallant officers. From August 17 to the end of September " D " Company had no officers (Lieutenant Hamilton having gone to hospital on account of his wound), and was under the command of Company Sergeant-Major Wm. Kee for about six weeks, when he got his commission and still retained command. It is common knowledge to

118

those in the regiment how well he shouldered the responsibility placed upon him during this trying period. He received the distinction of being mentioned in dispatches.

From this date open fighting at Suvla practically ceased. A standstill set in. To say that it was unwelcome would be untrue, for the inactivity after the severe fatigue and lack of rest was like a drink to a thirsty man. From the fire trenches that were occupied by the Dublins the ground, as may be seen from the contours, sloped away down a valley, on the farther side of which might be seen the Turkish trenches between the two spurs, on Scimitar Hill and Ismail Oglu Tepe. The outline of the trenches was quite visible in some places about five or six hundred yards distant. Scimitar Hill presented a burnt appearance, having been set on fire by the shelling on the 21st, and, as may be seen from the map, behind it lay the village of Biyuk Anafarta, which by this time was in ruins with the excellent practice of our naval guns. Farther to the right could be seen Ismail Oglu Tepe, against which the attack had been delivered. It seemed to be a complete network of trenches, many of which had been constructed in the face of the hill, which at places was almost perpendicular. Behind them could be seen the Sari Bair Mountains towering up to about a thousand feet. Here a foothold had been actually gained on August 8, but had to be relinquished on account of the failure of the Suvla Bay troops.

The weeks that followed were somewhat monotonous, sometimes in the firing-line, sometimes in reserve, but always full of danger, for the Dublins, like other regiments, were all the time under the fire of snipers or of shrapnel, which exacted a very heavy toll in casualties. They were also weeks of discomfort and debility, for during them disease became most rife. Work was incessant, as after the failure of the 21st the troops had been told that the trenches must be held at any cost as a breach at any point might bring disaster on the whole line. The position was very serious as there was no second line on which the troops could fall back. This made the holding of the first line imperative. Night after night the attack that never came was waited for. At much danger digging trenches and saps was carried on in front, barbed wire erected, scrub that gave cover cleared away, and trees hewn down—all by men of whom many were weakened by dysentery and disease.

Of this, their third week-end on the Peninsula, and a few days following, another writes :

"The following morning (Saturday, August 21) broke clear and fine, and our artillery both on land and sea replied to the Turkish batteries which had opened the ball previously, and the shells fell very close to us but did not do much harm. We stopped in our cover for the morning, and at one o'clock in a blazing sun the Fleet and all our land batteries began a bombardment of the neighbouring hills, which were held in force by the enemy and which we were to attack later. The bombardment lasted for over an hour, and at the end the hills were on fire in many places and it seemed impossible that any one could possibly be left alive there—the Turks had not once replied to our fire ; they were too ' cute.'

"About 3 p.m. on this blazing Saturday afternoon we got the order to prepare to advance, and as we got into our equipment and gave a last touch of oil to our best friend (the rifle), I can tell you that our hearts were going pit-a-pat, as we all knew well what awaited us as soon as we left our cover. However, not a soul hung back when the order came to advance—we defiled as smartly as on parade over the hill and took up our positions in the open in lines of companies. We advanced at a brisk pace across into

the open plains which lay at the bottom of the hills, and
until we had gone about a mile and a half there was no
notice taken of us by the enemy, except the snipers, who
were busy picking off the officers but without much
success, as the range was too long. However, things were
soon to hum. Just as we got nicely into the middle of a
great field, which had been ploughed up by the Turks to
render advancing more difficult, the enemy opened fire!

" Good Lord! They didn't half plop the shells into us—
shrapnel, high-explosive and lyddite shells were bursting
in absolute hundreds in front, above, and behind us, and
now and then to add intensity to their fire numerous land
mines blew up, throwing men and rocks into the air and
blinding us with sand. Men fell all around, and the
shouts and smell of the lyddite were awful. Soon the
air was laden with pungent smoke which caused great
smarting to the eyes, but those of us who were lucky
enough to be still unhurt advanced. When we got out
of the field the order to extend came, as we were now
under rifle-fire, and we advanced at the double, throwing
ourselves down as flat as possible every twenty-five yards
to get our breath, then : ' Prepare to advance. Advance! '
Up and away in a rush forward for another twenty-five
yards and down again. Our casualties were much more
heavy now, as the range was suitable to rifle-fire and the
Turks would wait until we were getting up, and at each
halt we left many men to mark our rests. Needless to
say I had many narrow escapes, and in one case I was
sent flying by a high-explosive shell which burst near
me. I got rather bruised, but was up again in a flash
and away after the advancing line—out of breath, but
otherwise unhurt.

" However, to make a long story short, we got there fairly
wet and dripping with perspiration. By Jove! It was

'some' enjoyment for a Saturday afternoon, but we dug
ourselves in behind a hedge and waited for nightfall and
reinforcements, and in a very short time, when we had
dug head-cover to safeguard our heads, we had a long
drink and then the blessings of a cigarette—of course the
Turks were banging away at us, but we knew we were
fairly safe, and we were so dead-beat that we didn't heed
them, because we knew they were on the run. Later
that night we advanced and took possession of a trench
which the Turks had deserted, and which we consolidated
and reconstructed for our own defence. About midnight
the enemy made a counter-attack, but they were mowed
down, and soon all was quiet save for a snap of a sniper's
rifle as a chap incautiously exposed himself. Those of
us who were not on watch were glad to lie down and smoke
and talk of those who had fallen until our watch came
round.

" Sunday morning (August 22) broke as glorious as usual
in these climes, and the Turks early commenced their
shelling of our position, but we took no notice except to
stoop behind the parapet when we heard the ' buzz ' of
a shell coming too near, and soon we had our mess-tins
on little fires, preparing for breakfast of black tea, bully
beef, and biscuits, which we thoroughly enjoyed.

" We were moved along the trenches and held the position
for several days, which were generally spent as follows :
An hour before dawn (about 3.45 or 4 a.m.) every man
' stands ' to his position, bayonet fixed and ready for an
attack, as the Turks generally attack at dawn, and when
their attack was beaten off, as it generally was, with few
casualties to us, the watches for the day were told off,
and those not going on guard immediately went off to
cook breakfast. After breakfast gangs were told off for
trench-digging, and for two hours each man dug in the

sap towards the enemy's lines. It was very tiring work, as we had to keep well bent all the time for fear of the snipers. The rest of the day generally passed quietly except for fatigues like bringing up water and rations.

"And when some days news flew along the trenches, 'There is a post in,' there would be a cheer and every one would shout, 'Any for me?' It is a great relief when one hears one's name shouted, and away down for the letters and parcels—Turks and all forgotten in the wild desire of news from home. I think if the people at home knew the inspiriting effect of a letter they would write every day.

"One of the worst duties I found was that of 'listening patrol.' A non-commissioned officer and about ten men climb over our own parapet and creep about half-way to the Turks' trenches and there lie down as flat as possible and listen to what goes on in the enemy's lines. This is to safeguard us against a rush from the enemy in the dark. One night I happened to be on this party, and when we had been out for about an hour the 'dam' moon got up and exposed us plainly to the Turks. Of course they soon got busy, and bullets tore up the ground all round us. For four hours we lay there, and I am not ashamed to say I never prayed so hard in my life. However, God was good, and we got back safe and sound, but very nervous."

On the evening of the 22nd they took up a position about a mile and a half to the right of Chocolate Hill, on the northern side of the Asmak Dere, towards Hetmanchair, and stayed until September 5 in the trenches there. During this period they were shifted still more to the north to make room for some Yeomanry regiment which took over the right of the line next the river. There they joined up with the Munsters until on September 5 they went back to the reserve camp on the higher slopes of Chocolate Hill for four or five days, during which they were under constant shell-fire.

Their experiences of life in this district were very severe. Water was exceedingly scarce, and few of the men got a wash during the whole period, while the dust, heat, and flies were almost unbearable. It was here that the most serious outbreak of dysentery arose. The following extract describes the flies at Suvla :

" . . . I must really pause here and enter a protest against the flies. The singular number, I understand, denotes one, and the plural more than one, but to describe the number of flies we have here would require a super-plural. It is not that we have merely ' more than one '—we have myriads of flies. And such enterprising flies ! They visit everything from dead Turks down. They light on your face. You knock them away, and, just as if they were attached to your face with elastic, they bump back again the moment you pick up the pencil."

The rum issue was one of the events which at first was all too rare. It was measured out to the platoon sergeant from a jar, and the quota for his men would be about a canteen and a half. The platoon sergeant then called his platoon together or went down the trench, and with a spoon ladled out the rum into cups, tins, canteens, and all kinds of receptacles. These tots were very welcome and put fresh life into the half-chilled men on awakening in the early morning, for the nights were becoming much colder.

On the whole, they did not complain of the food, but a word about it may not be out of place. After the first few days they appear to have been well supplied, as the following extracts show :

"*August* 18.—We are now getting plenty of food, and most of us have become expert cooks."

And another :

"*September* 16.—We are getting plenty of good food, and very much enjoy cooking over little fires in the trenches. We receive a ration of dry tea, sugar, and milk daily, and can make our tea in a tin whenever we like, and I am afraid we are getting to be great tea-drinkers, as it is so good. We also get sufficient tinned meats, biscuits, and occasionally jam and rice. . . . Sometimes bacon for breakfast, and sometimes onions and potatoes. . . . Occasionally I get a few figs off the numerous fig-trees that grow all over the place just like the beech-trees at home. We often come across melons, too, which are very fine. Vineyards are common here, but unfortunately they have no grapes at present."

When they went back to the seashore for a rest or a bathe it was worse than the firing-line, as the shelling was continuous on that place.

One of the company writes of his experiences in the trenches at this period as follows :

"I'll just give you a little account of the last time we were under big fire. It happened a few days ago just before we were relieved. Of course you understand that artillery-fire goes on the whole time, and that the big guns are never silent except at night, and that the cowardly snipers are popping away all day with explosive bullets that make ghastly wounds. Well, we had all just finished tea the other day when the Turks started to absolutely rain shells on our trenches. It was grand to see them burst—a bright flash and then a white fleecy cloud, as shrapnel burst; or a denser cloud as lyddite, common shell, or high explosive tore up holes in the ground. This, of course, means that it was in a different part of the line from where we were, otherwise it would not have been quite so grand, and I would not have been watching it, but crouching behind cover somewhere. Well, as I said, this was away on the left and right of us. We were in the centre, and, of course, as soon as the Turks started our guns absolutely tore the heavens to ribbons in reply. The naval guns also took a hand, and they are the business; without them we would never have had the ghost of a chance all along. The sound of them, firing from about four miles behind us, and then the heavy crash as they burst—like some one slamming a gigantic door six or seven hundred yards in front of us—is very comforting when you know they hardly ever miss. All this time, of course, we could hear the slow, leisurely tearing of the air, as the shrapnel went by us, or the harsh scream of the high explosive, both of our own guns and the enemy's trying to find our batteries and silence them. Some of the shells picked up on the beach have been found by the timepiece, that every shell has, to have been fired from ten miles off—so you see we get quite heavy enough guns here; they are not all in Flanders. Of course a shell that is meant for where you are yourself never gives you any warning, and you do not hear any tearing of the air or anything like that. All you hear is the 'bang' of the gun, and, simultaneously, there is a burst, and you wonder if you are still alive; this is shrapnel. If high explosive comes near there is a sort of miniature earthquake, and sometimes you see rocks, rifles, equipment, limbs, etc., all going up in the air, and there is a rush to repair the trench. Mind you, this very seldom happens, and only once have we been troubled, and that is the occasion I am telling you about. Well, we were quite enjoying the fun when suddenly rifle-fire, with its sharp crackle, like innumerable whips being cracked without ceasing, and the coughing of machine-guns, just like an asthmatical motor-bike, broke out all along the front. We all dived from the dug-outs and hurried into the fire trench, buckling on equipment and loosening ammunition. I had not my coat or puttees on, but I had my gun and bullets all serene. Well, for over half an hour bullets sang overhead, or thudded into the bank in front of us or the sandbags on top of the parapet. The ricochets, too, have a lovely hiss, worse than a thousand snakes, as they fly over one. We opened fire, of course, as we knew the direction of the trenches, but not a Turk did we see, and it all calmed down and was as quiet as ever. The story is that some ' big bug ' arrived down from Constantinople and he and all the Turkish Staff were on the side of the hills, and he had ordered an attack and was waiting to see us all swept back into the sea ; but our guns spotted where they had all their reinforcements massed and scattered them like the deuce. Anyway, when the word was given to attack, *eight* Turks got out of the trenches—and got back in a h—— of a hurry."

From the reserve trenches on Chocolate Hill they moved back to a so-called rest camp at Lala Baba on September 9. During the four days they were here (until the 13th) they were subjected to continual shell-fire, so much so that on one day they had thirty casualties. From this position they were moved round by Lala Baba and the Salt Lake to the front trenches at Ali Bey Chesme, to the north of Chocolate Hill, again joining up with the Munsters. Here they remained until September 21.

Incidents in their daily life were like the following :

THE PALS AT SUVLA BAY

"*All things considered*, I really must say we can't grumble, and if we once drive the Turks back far enough to leave the *Base* out of range, matters will rapidly improve. I don't really see much chance of that at present, but one can only hope for the best. These Turks are not at all considerate of one's comfort; a few days ago when I was enjoying another bath in a biscuit tin, the Turks had the audacity to make a surprise attack. Now it is bad enough to be clothed and in one's right mind on these occasions, but to be in one's birthday costume with one's thoughts in Dublin, well, *then* it becomes, to say the least of it, rather awkward; however, I grasped my rifle and bayonet, also some ammunition and began to fire away, then when they were driven back and when things had quietened down a bit, I began to dress, and then for the first time the fellows noticed me, and you should have heard them laugh.

"We had a fairly narrow shave in our dug-out a few days ago. We had just finished our tea in the evening when suddenly we heard the shriek of shrapnel shell coming uncomfortably close to us, and then a 'bang,' and we saw all the ground a few yards away riddled with bullets. So we thought it was time to get a move on, and we had no sooner got into our trench when 'bang' went another shell right into our dug-out. 'By heavens,' said one chap, 'they nearly got us that time.' After awhile we went back to see what damage was done, and you should have seen the dug-out—holes in water-bottles, oil-sheets, top-coats, and everything riddled and covered with clay."

How brave and cheery were their letters, making light of their terrible hardships—thirst, heat, flies, fierce fighting, monotonous food, and the wearying struggle against dysentery. One can only be filled with admiration and affection

128

for such men, who, amid it all, never failed in loyalty and comradeship to one another.

They were thankful for even the smallest comfort :

" Another chap and myself happened on a grand dug-out at the Rest Camp ; we have a bit of straw to sleep on, and when we slip off our boots it is quite like going to bed."

They would joke, no matter what happened :

" One chap was out the other day and a shrapnel shell burst pretty close to him, knocking his cigarette out of his mouth. ' Well,' says he, ' a joke is a joke, but when it comes to knocking a cigarette out of your mouth it is no joke.' "

A few more lines will end our story. From the trenches on Chocolate Hill they went back to the dug-outs about three hundred yards behind the firing-line, which they occupied until September 29, on which night they were supposed to move up again to the trenches. They received the order to be ready in the afternoon, but this was cancelled about 6 p.m., and their extra ammunition taken from them. They were told to keep one blanket and roll the others up in bundles. Shortly after midnight they were marched down to the beach at Lala Baba, and to their surprise put into lighters there and sent aboard a small transport, which sailed for Lemnos that night.

Of the original company there remained but seventy-nine to leave the Peninsula. As these survivors looked back from the transport at the scene of so much unavailing blood-shed, they were only human if they hoped that there might be some little recognition or word of praise for them. But it was not to be, save that in these pages an effort has been made to retrieve from oblivion the live human detail of their deeds. They with others may have failed in accomplishing all that was placed before them. Looking back it still seems to them to have been an impossible task that was set, but they faced it cheerfully and gave of their best to achieve the goal. *Spectamur agendo*—We judge them by their deeds. As they steamed away into the darkness every one's heart was saddest at the thought of leaving their courageous dead on the hill-sides and cliffs that they were abandoning, but to their comrades and their friends the memory of all they did and tried to do will never fade. The lines of Kipling come to mind :

> " *Not easy hope or lies*
> *Shall bring us to our goal,*
> *But iron sacrifice*
> *Of body, will and soul.*
> *There's but one task for all ;*
> *For each one life to give ;*
> *Who stands if freedom fall ?*
> *Who dies, if England live ?* "

CHAPTER X

THE CHAPLAINS AND THE WOUNDED

SO far in this narrative we have not mentioned either of the two excellent chaplains who accompanied the Dublins, Canon M'Clean, Rector of Rathkeale, Co. Limerick, and the Rev. Father Murphy, of the Curragh, Co. Kildare. As embodying what the men thought of them, we may give extracts from two letters written about this period of the operations:

" *Thursday, September* 23.—Good morning. We are in the reserve trenches at present and have been here since Tuesday night, when we came down from the firing-line. I am not sure how long we stay here, but either for four or eight days and then back to the firing-line. Well, to go on about that service. The service was held by Canon M'Clean just in the reserve trenches. The only clerical robes he had were the black band that was thrown across the shoulders of his service jacket. We first sang a hymn, then went through the service just as at night-time in the Mariners. The Canon preached a short but moving sermon. It takes a lot to move some of the Tommies, and you can imagine it must have been more than a good sermon when I tell you that although we were not kept ten minutes there were tears in the eyes of most of us, though I myself was admiring the Canon more than his sermon. Canon M'Clean is well over fifty years of age—a fine, well-built, grey-headed old fellow, the best-natured and most cheerful soul you ever came across. I suppose there is not a man in the battalion who would not willingly give his life for him. How he sticks the life God only knows, but, nevertheless, he sticks it as well as any of us, and let us hope, D.V., he will continue to do so. Father Murphy, who is his boon companion, is just the same type of man only about ten years younger, and two more Christian gentlemen no one ever came across."

And another as follows :

" The weather is now beginning to get cooler, but the flies are abominable. They would plague a saint. Father Murphy said Mass on Sunday, and I received Holy Communion ; he is admired by all. The Mass and the conditions under which it was celebrated will prove interesting conversation when we meet again."

Here is one from an officer, which speaks of both :

" I really must say something about Father Murphy and Canon M'Clean, the Church of Ireland minister. These are our clergymen of the 6th and 7th Dublins and 6th and 7th Munsters, which four battalions form the 30th Brigade.

" This morning Father Murphy said Mass in the trenches, where bullets, etc., were falling like hailstones. Oh ! he is a splendid man.

" The Canon, a dear old Irishman, from Limerick, holds his service side by side with Father Murphy. They put a great spirit into the men, who love them both, in fact almost adore them. I personally think that nothing is good enough for these two noble gentlemen. Catholic and Protestant are hand in hand, all brought about by the gentleness and undaunted courage displayed by these two splendid soldiers of Christ.

CHAPLAINS AND WOUNDED

" Never since the landing has the roar of battle, be it ever so ferocious (and God knows it is bad here at times), prevented these clergymen from forcing their way into the firing-line and attending to our gallant sons of Ireland."

And Brigadier-General Nicol, commanding the 30th Brigade, wrote to Canon M'Clean when the latter was temporarily invalided through ill-health : " I hope sincerely for our sakes that you will get back to us, though you have done your share in this war—and nobly, too. We of the 30th Brigade are never likely to forget your fearless devotion to your duty. With you and Father Murphy we were indeed fortunate, and it was so splendid to see you two the best of friends, working hand in hand for the common good. You both set us a fine example."

What higher testimony to Christian character and devotion to duty could these two clergymen receive than that contained in these letters of the general, officers, and men of the 30th Brigade.

Each of them has been requested to prepare from his diary an account of his ministrations during the campaign, which shall be given in his own words.

Canon MClean writes :

" I should like, in the first instance, to pay a tribute to my constant companion and colleague, the Rev. Father Murphy. We were together from the formation of the 30th Brigade at the Curragh, through Basingstoke, and practically through the whole of the Suvla Bay campaign. I cannot express the admiration and affection that I have always felt for his sterling character and lovable disposition. We occupied the same tents, we lived in the same dug-outs, and we held services in the trenches side by side. He was my constant adviser and friend in health and sickness and was always looking after me. The affection I had for him was shared by officers and men of all ranks in the brigade.

" The question has often been asked, How did the chaplains manage to have services for the men of their respective Churches ? Naturally the circumstances were quite different from what is experienced at home. With very few exceptions it was impossible to have a parade service near the firing-line. Owing to the number of hostile aeroplanes that were continually scouting, the men on parade would be exposed to immediate shell-fire.

" The alternative was to take the men in the trenches by battalion and have celebrations of the Holy Communion. The officiating chaplain wore no vestments over his uniform, only a stole, as anything white would attract snipers' fire. He brought all the Elements consecrated.

" Unless an engagement was going on I visited the trenches and went through the battalions about three times a week and had services for any units which I could not reach on Sunday. Thus, as a rule, I managed to have a service weekly for each battalion apart from Sunday services. It was my custom to go up to the trenches on Saturday after having a celebration of Holy Communion at the Ambulance and call on my way at the Brigade Headquarters and arrange for the service there at 9.30 a.m. for General Staff and Head-quarter troops.

" On reaching the firing-line where the Tenth Division was placed, I saw the commanding officer of each battalion and arranged the hour of services for Sunday. I stayed the night in trenches.

" I usually commenced with an 8.30 service for one of the battalions. I selected one of the firing platforms in the centre of the battalion and there put up my portable altar, and word was sent down the line for all belonging to the Church of England to attend. The officers and men knelt in the trenches as near as possible to me. I had a shortened Communion Service and walked down the trench administering the Holy Communion. I thus managed to have four services before 12.30 p.m.

"My Sunday work was not yet finished, as shortly after 2 p.m. I had to set out for the Division Headquarters, which was between two and three miles away, and had service there; then on to my Ambulance and had evening service, and so ended my Sunday's work.

"On Monday morning I again started for the trenches and had service for any battalion I was unable to reach on Sunday.

"I landed with the 7th Munsters at Suvla Point, Gallipoli, on August 7, 1915. The Dublins landed near Lala Baba, marched round the promontory and crossed the Salt Lake to attack Chocolate Hill. Thus our brigade was split up— the 6th and 7th Munsters and Field Ambulance to the left of Suvla Bay, the 6th and 7th Dublins to the right about four miles away. I was ordered to go with the Munsters. On August 13 the 6th and 7th Dublins joined the Munsters at Karakol Dagh preparatory to their attack on Kiretch Tepe Sirt. It was on Friday they joined up; the two battalions were side by side resting, and I went through the battalions and spoke to the officers and men of the 7th Dublins. I knew the men of the 'D' Company best. My organist, Private Elvery, choir leader, Private Coldwell, and choir for the 30th Brigade were all of the 'D' Company. I can only express here my gratitude and thanks for their assistance and loyal co-operation from the first battalion service I held at Basingstoke on through the Suvla and Servian campaign—they never failed me, even in the most trying circumstances. The Dublins were on the reserve at this time, viz. August 14, and Munsters in the firing-line.

"On Friday, August 13, I managed to have an open-air

Holy Communion for the 6th Munsters. I had four officers and one hundred and fifty men at it on a slope of the hill near where the fighting was going on. We were in a sheltered place, and the snipers' bullets whizzed harmlessly over our heads. On Saturday, the 14th, during a lull in the fighting I went into the front trenches, which are held by the 7th Munsters, and had a most encouraging celebration of Holy Communion in a 'kloof' at the end of the trenches near the sea. I had a hundred men, with officers—all that could be spared from duty. Unfortunately, after leaving service, two men were sniped, one slightly, and the other more seriously wounded.

"The 30th Brigade held the left of the line, which extended about four miles. On Sunday, the 15th, I had a celebration at Divisional Headquarters for Lord Granard's Pioneer Regiment. This battalion is recruited largely from Limerick. There are about three hundred Churchmen in the regiment. I had two hundred communicants. I had arranged for a service for the 6th and 7th Dublins at Headquarters of the brigade at 11.30 a.m., but only a company of each were able to attend, as an attack was to take place at 12.30. I had a short parade service and Holy Communion for any that desired afterwards. I had a dozen officers and men. Afterwards I went forward with the regiment into action, and from behind one of the Maxim-gun shelters saw the brilliant charge of the 6th Dublins and the 6th Munsters. The hill was taken at the point of the bayonet. It was a wonderful sight to see the men deploying in open order, the cheers and charge—the men in the cruiser manned the decks and the rigging and cheered; naturally we lost men in taking the position, which was a very important one, and soon the wounded were brought by on stretchers. I was with Captain Preston and Lieutenant Richards, who later died of their wounds, and I buried both of them next day beside

AN OFFICER'S GRAVE, KARAKOL DAGH

FATHER MURPHY GIVING GENERAL ABSOLUTION
TO THE 6TH AND 7TH DUBLINS, AUGUST 15

ON KARAKOL DAGH

ON KARAKOL DAGH

(*Father Murphy in centre*)

CHAPLAINS AND WOUNDED

Lieutenant Travers, a machine-gun officer of the 7th Munsters, who was killed a few days before. We took a good many Turkish prisoners and one German officer.

"It is marvellous how one gets accustomed to rifle- and shell-fire. Shells were bursting all round the 31st Field Ambulance, but we were all in dug-outs which shelter us from the shrapnel. I saw, one evening, two German Taubes throwing bombs on our battleships, the latter firing anti-aircraft shells at them; the next evening I saw our airships spying out the Turks and being shelled, the Fleet firing at the same time high-explosive shells over our heads, and the Turks replying; in fact, one got so accustomed to this heavy firing that one did not notice it. All day and night the rattle of the rifle-fire and the 'whirr' of the Maxim-guns and the explosion of shells were going on.

"I had a hard day on Monday, the 16th, seeing the wounded from 6 a.m. till midnight. On Tuesday morning I went up at 4 a.m. to near the firing-line, as I heard that a lot of cases were at the 1st Field Dressing Station. I arrived there about 5 a.m. and was soon under dropping bullets and snipers' fire. Ministered to the wounded.

"Going up the hill a man behind me was shot through the head. I was sniped at three times—a bullet just grazed my head, and while lying down behind a rock two bullets struck just over my head. I finally took refuge with the medical officer of the 7th Dublins, and had to stay there three hours owing to the sweeping of the hill-side by high-explosive shells.

"If a regiment is near the firing-line, the men at once dig themselves in and erect shelters of various kinds, otherwise a man would have no chance of his life. It is marvellous how cool our men were, and as for their bravery no one could imagine it unless one saw it. The difficulty was to make men take cover.

THE PALS AT SUVLA BAY

" During the following week I visited the 7th Dublins and gave Holy Communion to the officers and men. I had close on two hundred communicants. From that time I was in close touch with the 7th Dublins right through the campaign. I find from my notebook that on Friday, August 20, I was up with the 30th Brigade and had Holy Communion at 9 a.m. for 7th Dublins, 6th Dublins, and 6th Munsters. I had all the officers and one hundred and eighty men. At 3 p.m. all the battleships and batteries opened a most terrific bombardment ; soon the answering shells dropped all along the shore. I had a most miraculous escape ; a shell burst near me, the fuse flew over my head and killed a man near by. I then returned to the Ambulance.

" I went out at 8 p.m. on the night of Saturday, August 21, to the trenches, about four miles away, and spent the night with the 7th Dublins. There was a very heavy attack going on and I found it impossible to hold service on Sunday, the 22nd, so I returned from the trenches to the Ambulance, which I found on the move nearer to the sea beach. I was busy the whole of Monday with our wounded, and on Tuesday night, the 24th, I set out for the trenches with Captain Aplin of 7th Munsters, who was slightly wounded. We were sniped so heavily within a mile of the trenches that we had to make rushes of sixty yards or so and lie down, and when rested to go on again. In that manner we ultimately reached the trenches. I stayed the night with Major Hoey of 7th Dublins. Firing was going on all night and we got no sleep.

" On Wednesday morning word was sent along the line to the 6th and 7th Dublins that I was going to have Holy Communion for Church of England troops.

" I took them in batches of thirty at a time at different places in the trench. I find in my notebook that I had seventy communicants alone out of ' D ' Company of 7th

138

Dublins. I was able to give Holy Communion to the other battalion afterwards. I find by my notebook that we had only seventeen officers now out of one hundred and twenty in the Brigade. I spent Thursday at the Ambulance and had services for men, saw the wounded, and buried the dead.

"On Friday, the 27th, I went up at 6.30 p.m. to the Brigade. The Turks began shelling, and my orderly and I had finally to take refuge at the advanced dressing-station. I was advised to stay the night there, but determined to push on. On leaving the station we came immediately under heavy rifle-fire from the Turks. The dressing-station was a mile behind the trenches. When I got near my destination I made the last rush, and in doing so narrowly escaped being shot by the sentry. He challenged me three times, but I did not hear him owing to the heavy rifle- and shell-fire. Happily, he just recognized me before I jumped into the trench. I stayed with Captain Wilkinson of 7th Dublins. No sleep. The men and officers stood to arms all night.

" The next day, Saturday, the 28th, I had service for 7th Munsters at 11 a.m., and after that for 7th Dublins at 11.45. There were a hundred communicants out of 7th Dublins. I stayed Saturday night with 6th Dublins, gave them celebration at 8.30 a.m. on Sunday morning, and went to Brigade Headquarters and gave Holy Communion to General Nicol, Staff, and fifty men; afterwards went to 6th Munsters, got back to Ambulance at 12. Had service there at 12.30; then Divisional Headquarters at 5.30. Returned ill to camp, and ordered to stay in camp for three days' rest by commanding officer.

" Thus my work went on during our stay in Gallipoli.

" We left Suvla Bay early in October and landed at Mudros for so-called rest. We stayed only three days there. I was able to have a parade service for battalions on October 3. We landed at Salonika on October 8.

THE PALS AT SUVLA BAY

"I will always look back with happiness to the months I acted as chaplain to the 30th Brigade. The kindness, consideration, and help I got from officers and men is deeply engraved on my heart. The deep religious spirit manifested by all was so helpful; the services were voluntary, yet no man was absent except on duty. Many a time after service the men of the 'D' Company came round me and said, 'Come soon again.' With such officers and men one felt that one's strength and life was at the service of real heroes."

Father Murphy writes:

"My spiritual charge consisted of the four battalions of the 30th Infantry Brigade, namely, the 6th and 7th Battalions of the Royal Dublin Fusiliers and the 6th and 7th Battalions of the Royal Munster Fusiliers. I was attached to the Royal Dublin Fusiliers for the outward journey. We had Mass and Holy Communion on board ship daily, on week-days at 6.45 a.m.; on Sundays at 7 a.m. and 9 a.m.

"In Mudros Harbour, under date July 23 to 24, I find this happening recorded: 'Nesbitt paraded the officers of the 6th and 7th Royal Dublin Fusiliers for confession at midnight.' Poor Nesbitt belonged to the 6th Royal Dublin Fusiliers.

"We next anchored in the beautiful harbour of Mitylene.

"On leaving the Royal Dublin Fusiliers to join up with the Royal Munster Fusiliers at Mudros, I find the following entry: 'Very sorry parting with Dublins. Nearly all came to confession and got my blessing before I started. It was like leaving home again parting with them.'

"I landed at Suvla with the Royal Munster Fusiliers. The 6th and 7th Royal Dublin Fusiliers, after fighting in the Salt Lake region, joined us on August 13. My diary reads: '*August* 13.—Visited 6th and 7th Royal Dublin

Fusiliers Battalions (just arrived) on top of Karakol Dagh. Gave them a general absolution.

"'*August* 15, *Sunday* (*Lady Day*).—Started from Ambulance to bivouac of Dublins and Munsters on Karakol Dagh at 4 a.m. Said Mass for them respectively at 6 and 7 a.m. Gave a general absolution. Quite a number for Holy Communion. Visited men along the lines afterwards whose duty kept them from Mass. Gave them absolution and Holy Communion. Had decided to spend week-end on the hill with them, when orders arrived after 1 p.m. to fall in for battle. Then visited each regiment singly, said prayers and gave them absolution just as they marched into the fight.

"'*August* 16.—Found chaplains and medical men busy at Ambulance.

"'*August* 17.—Went up with stretcher-party to advanced dressing-station at 9 p.m., and returned at 5 a.m. to Ambulance. The wounded of two brigades, the 29th and 30th, were collected in two tents on the hill, which was swept by rifle-fire. It was affecting to see these poor fellows bearing their wounds *more solito* with the greatest fortitude. Hardly a sound beyond a suppressed moan broke the stillness. *A peste, bello et fame, libera nos Domine.*

"'18*th*.—Attempted with Canon M'Clean to reach brigade. Night fell and we had to return. He is a splendid colleague.

"'19*th*.—When firing ceased went to brigade in "rest camp"—so-called. Said Rosary on hill-side, which falls almost sheer into sea. Then gave absolution to 7th Royal Dublin Fusiliers, etc.

"'21*st*.—Learned Brigade had moved. Was starting with M'Clean at 2.45 for advanced dressing-station on Lala Baba, when artillery duel started so fierce that we took to our dugouts. Made again for Lala Baba 7 p.m. with orderly, and stayed night.

"'22*nd*.—M'Clean was the first object my eyes lit on

before 5 a.m. He had wandered in all sorts of weird places during the night. We both spent a few hours on hospital ship chock-full of wounded and made a round of patients. Got back to our starting-place of previous evening to find the ambulance trekking towards pontoon about 6.30 p.m. Our journey all the way was to shrapnel accompaniment. Clouds of sand drew the fire on us. Headed off again to advanced dressing-station after dinner.

" ' 23rd.—Chaplains were from this onward at Ambulance on beach. Brigade about an hour's journey inland.

" ' 25th.—Went to front trenches 8 p.m. Slept overnight in trench of advanced medical aid post. Snipers galore. Made for Dublins and Munsters over four hundred yards of exposed country, 8 a.m. Heard confession of 7th Royal Dublin Fusiliers, etc.

" ' 26th.—Boarded hospital ship with Canon, made round of sick and wounded.

" ' 29th.—Mass 7 a.m. on beach. Aeroplane dropped bomb, Knocked out seven, of whom two very seriously.

" ' 30th.—Captain Hoey, now Commanding Officer 7th Royal Dublin Fusiliers, has been a patient. Made with him for trenches, 8.45 a.m. Got into thick of shrapnel shelling. No cover, lay low; faced music again at 10 a.m., this time in peace. Gave Holy Communion to 7th Royal Dublin Fusiliers.

" ' 31st.—Boarded hospital ship with Canon. Made round of wounded.

" ' Indisposed for these few days, September 1 to 5.

" ' *September* 7.—Gave absolution to 7th Royal Dublin Fusiliers on Chocolate Hill.

" ' 12th.—Mass and Holy Communion, 7th Royal Dublin Fusiliers at Lala Baba.

" ' 22nd.—Holy Communion to half the 7th Royal Dublin Fusiliers in reserve trenches.

" ' *26th.*—Attempted to give Holy Communion to 7th Royal Dublin Fusiliers, but on reaching trenches shelling was too heavy. At request of commanding officer I deferred the service.

" ' *27th.*—Holy Communion at 7th Royal Dublin Fusiliers about a mile beyond Chocolate Hill.

" ' *October* 3.—Mass and Holy Communion for the Brigade at Lemnos.'

" I had been ailing during the last three weeks on the Peninsula, and on October 6 went sick.

" ' Left Peninsula night of October 31 to November 1.' "

It would only harrow the feelings to describe in detail the shock and suffering of the wounded. This has been brought keenly home to many. They lay where they fell, waiting and calling for water or a stretcher. If able, they crawled nearer the ambulance men. Nearly always they helped each other, the man who had lost his sight (and there were some) being guided by his comrade who needed support for his shattered shoulder-blade. In cases of lighter wounds they had to make their way to the dressing-station on the beach as best they could by night or day. One instance is as good as twenty to let us know what the journey to the base hospital was like :

" He helped me to get a stretcher from the Royal Army Medical Corps which would take me to the base. I eventually got one, and during my voyage I was dropped like a hot potato every few hundred yards while the stretcher-bearers ran under cover from shell-fire. It was better to have one man killed than three. I got to the base about 11 a.m., and I lay in the sun there, not able to move until evening, by which time hundreds of wounded men were being brought along. At about 6 p.m. a high-explosive shell landed right in the middle of the base hospital, and there were a number hit by pieces of the shell, so with all possible speed we were hurried on to the beach and we lay there all night until 8 a.m. the next morning, when we were put on board a small boat which took us out to the hospital ship."

Of course many a fine fellow had found his grave in the deep, the result of wounds or dysentery. The feelings of the wounded were akin to those of the wounded soldier returning from France :

> " *Back again! Back again!*
> *Out o' mud and blood and rain :*
> *Out o' gun-sound,*
> *God A'mighty,*
> *Out o' Blazes and home to ' Blighty ' !*
> *Broke right up and full o' pain,*
> *But back again—back again!* "

APPENDIX

APPENDIX

LIST OF OFFICERS AND MEN OF 7TH ROYAL DUBLIN FUSILIERS MENTIONED IN DISPATCHES OF SIR IAN HAMILTON FOR DISTINGUISHED GALLANTRY IN THE FIELD AT SUVLA BAY

Lieutenant-Colonel G. DOWNING.
Major R. S. M. HARRISON (killed).
Major M. P. E. LONSDALE.
Captain (temporary Major) C. B. R. HOEY, Adjutant.
Temporary Captain R. P. TOBIN (killed).
Temporary Captain L. S. N. PALMER.
Temporary Captain G. N. WILKINSON.
No. 14153, Regimental Sergeant-Major A. GUEST.
No. 14132, Company-Sergeant-Major W. KEE.
No. 14150, Sergeant A. E. BURROWES.
No. 14645, Sergeant E. C. MILLAR (killed).
No. 13852, Private A. E. WILKIN (killed).

D.C.M.

No. 14153, Acting Sergeant-Major A. GUEST, 7th Battalion Royal Dublin Fusiliers.

For conspicuous gallantry at Suvla Bay on the night of August 15–16, 1915, when he took ammunition out to the firing-line under heavy fire. He also located some snipers, and, advancing beyond the line at great risk, shot them.

THE PALS AT SUVLA BAY

COMPLETE ROLL IN NUMERICAL ORDER OF "D" COMPANY, 7TH ROYAL DUBLIN FUSILIERS

HARRISON, N.
O'DONNELL, J.
BROOKSBANK, W.
HICKEY, E. F.
KEESHAM, M. J.
COYNE, J.
HARE, E. H.
BOURKE, T. L.
McLACHLAN, E. B.
DENNEHY, P. J.
DARCUS, F. E.
WILKIN, A. E.
BAKER, C.
McCULLAGH, R. R.
WOODMAN, C.
BURNS, R. H.
POOLE, H.
SYNNOTT, E. F.
DRUMMOND, D.
MURRAY, W. C.
VERDON, E. H.
ROSS, F. A.
ISAAC, D. H.
FREEMAN, G. J.
KEE, W.
ROBERTSON, W. H.
ELVERY, J. W.
MATHEWS, W. F. A.
FALKINER, F. E. B.
KELLER, C. C.
EGAN, A. F.
RONALDSON, G. E.
PARRY, S. K.
WOODMAN, W. J. A.

GOURLAY, W. N.
BURROWES, A. E.
ENGLAND, A. J.
GUEST, A.
KENT, A. V.
CROOKSHANK, A. C.
CROOKSHANK, H.
BOURKE, R. S.
BRIGHT, H. S.
BELL, C. F. J.
HORNER, G. S.
BOYD, W. ST. C.
HARE, G.
McCARTHY, J. P.
GIBSON, H. W.
ARMSTRONG, R.
STRAHAN, A. H.
PECK, H. J.
BOURKE, E. C.
DOWSE, H. H.
CUNNIAM, J. F.
FAUSSET, V. H.
FIELD, S. H.
MARRABLE, F. A.
YOUNG, W. J.
MURRAY, A. H.
DOWSE, C. E.
LEA, A. V.
COX, J. F.
MOSS, A. W.
ANDERSON, H.
WINTER, J. A.
CASH, W. S.
STEPHEN, W. C.

PAUL, W. C.
SARGAISON, W. H.
DALE, T. S.
BRYCE, J.
FINDLATER, H. S.
FINDLATER, C. A.
MURPHY, R. V.
WHITTY, T. A.
BROWN, J. F. W.
ALEXANDER, G. G.
BLACK, T. S. C.
KEATING, J. J.
ENNIS, C. F. K.
PAUL, C. A.
COLDWELL, E. G.
BRIDGE, W. P.
SWAN, R. S.
SYMES, T. A.
BROOKS, H. B. J.
BOYD, H.
PERRY, J. J.
TAIT, W.
SHEIL, C.
STOKES, J. J.
HEATLEY, E. N.
BRADY, A.
POULTER, H. C.
GORDON, J.
POULTER, E. A.
BLACKMORE, P. B
BARRETT, E. R.
BAYLEY, J. U.
REID, W. S.
QUINN, R. P.

148

APPENDIX

HENRY, C. L.
FISHER, C. G. C.
JEFFRESON, V.
BLACK, F. J.
BROWN, N. W.
SUTCLIFFE, R. S.
HILLHOUSE, R. F.
ARTHURS, G. C.
JEEVES, C. A. V.
SAVILLE, C. A.
MACDONALD, C. J.
O'SULLIVAN, G. R.
MCCLELLAND, W.
EWEN, A. M.
CLEMENTS, W. H.
CARPENTER, J. H.
MCFERRAN, W. R.
DAVEY, R. B.
MEES, A. J.
PROSSER, J. H.
LOOKER, A. N.
MILLAR, E. C.
FINDLATER, C. A.
O'NEILL, C.
CRANWILL, G. B.
BRADY, J.
DALTON, A.
SCOTT, A.
RAINFORD, G. H.
CLARKE, J. F.
OLDHAM, E. A. S.
PIGOTT, A. C.
GABBE, E.
CORRELL, W. J.
MOUNT, W. J.
GUNNING, F. D.
MCALLEN, H.
ROBERTS, J. W.
HARPER, F. L.

HICKEY, C.
GLYNN, E.
GUNNING, G. C.
KARNEY, G. W.
FORBES, A.
GRAY, E. R.
MCCORMICK, D. N.
D'ALTON, M. J.
ALMOND, C. S.
BLACKMORE, T.
LATIMER, H. G.
PRICE, J. L.
RICHARDSON, M. P. V.
LITTLE, J. W.
MITCHELL, J.
LEE, C. G.
APPLEYARD, W. D'A.
SHAW, J. H. DE B.
MACAULEY, H. T. B.
CRADDOCK, J. J.
JACKSON, W.
NORMAN, C. G.
MORRISON, H. ST. J. R.
TAYLOR, A. McC.
SELFE, E. A. W.
EVANS, R. R.
DOLAN, G.
BURNS, R.
MACLAREN, W.
MORAN, M. J.
WAKEFIELD, W.
BRACKLEY, R. J.
USHER, W. H.
CLERY, W. J. O'F.
HARDING, S. W.
NAGLE, W. J.
CAMPBELL, S. W.
CATHIE, D. C.
PERROTT, F. W.

ATKINSON, W. H.
GRAY, W. V.
CLARKE, G. A.
MAY, A. E.
WATTS, S. C.
DARLING, S. G.
SHEPPARD, S.
WILLIAMS, T.
RIDOUT, G. H.
COX, J. F.
GUY, J. W.
KING, A. W.
HENRY, A. R.
MILLAR, E. C.
COFFEY, W.
ATTRIDGE, J. C.
CONNOLLY, R. W.
JENKINS, T. R.
BOYD, F. E.
HOWDEN, F. W.
DOOLEY, C. H.
GUILFOYLE, E.
WHELAN, J.
O'LOUGHLIN, M. M.
GRANT, J.
MCELLIGOTT, F.
MURRAY, T. R.
DAVIDSON, J. J.
POULTON, G. V.
THOMPSON, F. R.
ELLIOTT, T. C. M.
BLOUNT, A. M.
KERR, D.
PARKES, F. C. O'G.
WOODS, W. W.
ARMSTRONG, C. M.
CURTIS, T. C. M.
JOHN, P. R.
BALL, C. F.

THE PALS AT SUVLA BAY

CARRIG, T. B.	ROBERTS, H.	SHERWOOD, T. B.
PHILIPPE, D. G.	BOURKE, E.	MAY, J. P.
PHILLIPS, F. N.	O'DONNELL, M. M.	EVANS, J. A.
ALEXANDER, P. A.	GALLAGHER, G.	CREAGH, R. J.
MCCARTHY, W. T.	HAZLITT, J. B.	FORD, R. G. J.
NOLAN, E. W.	CALWELL, W. M.	HANNA, J. E.
DIXON, T. V.	MEREDITH, A. C.	BOYD, J.
ROBB, G. F.	MYLES, F.	HOLLAND, L.
CARMODY, G.	GREGOR, W. J.	EASTWOOD, J. W.
REID, R. F.	HEALY, J. J.	HICKMAN, T. O'B.
MCMURTRY, A. D.	SCALES, R. D.	MANNING, W. J.
DONOVAN, J. W. C.	TAVINER, H.	BAILEY, C.
HICKMAN, N. W. G.	KARNEY, D. N.	BULL, J.
FARRELLY, M.	BRADBURNE, E. S.	REDDY, T. F.
GARNHAM, J. H.	ADAMS, H. J.	DUFFEY, A. H.
JOHN, W. R.	ELKAN, H.	ROBINSON, F. J.
PENNEFATHER, R. K.	DUDLEY, H. P.	HUNTER, A. P.
ALLEN, W.	POLLOCK, H. C.	JENKINS, C. E.
KAVANAGH, H. A.	LAIRD, F. M.	WALKEY, F. A.
MAHER, P. J.	MCCARTHY, L.	MCCARTHY, J. P.
JORDAN, C. H.	COLLINS, J.	

OFFICERS

Company Commander
Captain POOLE H. HICKMAN

Company Second-in-Command
Captain R. P. TOBIN

Platoon Officers
Second-Lieutenant H. LECKY
Second-Lieutenant C. J. HAMILTON
Second-Lieutenant A. G. CRICHTON

P.S.—The Company was one platoon commander short ; but owing to the high standard of the non-commissioned officers, the commanding officer was satisfied to leave it so.

150

APPENDIX

MACHINE-GUN SECTION

MEMBERS OF " D " COMPANY TRANSFERRED TO " B " FOR MACHINE-GUN SECTION

DOUGLAS, R. G.	HOUSTON, T.	MATHEWS, W. F. A.
MACDONALD, C. J.	JENKINS, C. E.	MCFERRAN, W. R.
BRETT, J. T.	KEESHAM, M. J.	MURRAY, A. H.
CLARKE, J. R. R.	SCOTT, A.	ROBERTS, H.
CROOKSHANK, H.	SHANAGHER, D. P.	TAIT, W.
DODD, F. J.	WEATHERILL, E. T.	THOMPSON, F. R.
EXSHAW, R. L.	YOUNG, W. J.	MARRABLE, F. A.
FRAZER, D. M.	FALKINER, F. E. B.	

LIST OF THE SEVENTY-NINE MEN AND NON-COMMISSIONED OFFICERS, THE SURVIVORS OF " D " COMPANY, WHO LEFT SUVLA ON SEPTEMBER 29, 1915

No. 13 PLATOON

No. 1 SECTION

Sgt. Dale, T. S.
Pte. Brackley, R. J.
„ Reid, R. F.
„ Heatley, W.
„ Dooley, C. H.
„ Collins, J.

No. 2 SECTION

L.-C. Norman, C. G.
Pte. Fisher, C. G C.
„ Philippe, D. G.
„ Guy, J. W.
„ Gunning, G. C.

No. 3 SECTION

L.-C. Kavanagh, H. A.
Sgt. O'Donnell, M. F.
Pte. McCormick, D. N.
„ May, A. E.
„ Duffey, A. H.
„ Stephen, W. C.

No. 4 SECTION

Cpl. Forbes, A.
L.-C. Forbes, E. A.
„ Henry, C. L.
„ Gray, E. R.
Pte. Macaulay, A.
„ Ridout, G. H.
„ Selfe, E. A. W.
„ Reid, W. S.
„ Barrett, E. R.

No. 14 PLATOON

No. 5 SECTION

Sgt. Ross, F. A.
Cpl. Perry, J. J.
Pte. Baker, C. A.
„ Freeman, G. J.

No. 6 SECTION

L.-C. Robertson, W. H.
Pte. Alexander, G. G.
„ Farrelly, M.

No. 7 SECTION

L.-C. Ennis, C. F. K.
Pte. Glynn, E.
„ Moran, M. J.

No. 8 SECTION

Pte. Hanna, J. E.
„ Dando, G.
„ Burns, R.
„ Dolan, G.
„ Perrott, F. W.

No. 15 PLATOON

No. 9 SECTION

Sgt. Elvery, J. W.
Cpl. Woodman, W. J. A.
L.-C. Reddy, T. F.
Pte. Gourlay, W. N.
„ Woodman, C.
„ Manning, W. J.

151

THE PALS AT SUVLA BAY

No. 10 Section
L.-C. Mitchell, J.
Pte. Blount, A. M.
„ Meredith, A. C.
„ McCormick, D. N.

No. 11 Section
L.-C. Murphy, R. V.
Pte. Bright, H. S.
„ Armstrong, R.

No. 12 Section
L.-C. Hickman, N. W.
G.
Pte. Blackmore, I.
„ Nolan, E. W.
„ Davey, R. B.

No. 16 PLATOON

No. 13 Section
Sgt. O'Donnell, J.
Cpl. McMurtry, A. D.
Pte. Boyd, F. E.
„ Lee, C. G.
„ Jenkins, T. R.
„ Howden, F. W.
„ Henry, A. R.

No. 14 Section
L.-C. Harper, F. L.
Pte. Campbell, S. L.
„ May, J. P.
„ Hazlitt, J. B.
„ Willis, J.
„ McCarthy, J. P.

No. 15 Section
L.-C. Nagle, W. J.
Pte. Craddock, J. J.
„ McAllen, H.
„ McCullagh, R. R.
„ O'Loughlin, M.M.

No. 16 Section
Pte. Jackson, W.
„ Keesham, M. J.
„ Carrig, F. B.
„ Clery, W. J. O'F.
„ Oldham, E. A. S.
„ McElligott, F.

Platoon Sergeants
(13) Dale, T. S.
(14) Ross, F. A.
(15) Elvery, J. W.
(16) O'Donnell, J.

"D" COMPANY, 7th ROYAL DUBLIN FUSILIERS RECORD COMMITTEE

Chairman
F. H. Browning, Esq.*

Hon. Treasurer
Lieutenant-Colonel R. F. Tobin, R.A.M.C., F.R.C.S.I.

Hon. Secretary
Henry Hanna, Esq., K.C.

C. H. Crookshank, Esq.
Sergeant J. D'Alton, 7th R.D.F.
Rev. Canon Dowse, M.A.
A. Marrable, Esq.

E. J. McElligott, Esq., K.C.
H. J. Millar, Esq.
H. W. Moss, Esq.
A. Weatherill, Esq.

* On the death of Mr. Browning, Lieutenant-Colonel Tobin was elected Chairman of the Committee.

RECRUITS FOR "D" COMPANY, 7TH ROYAL DUBLIN FUSILIERS, LANSDOWNE ROAD, SEPTEMBER 1914

SERGEANT-MAJOR GUEST AND MR. F H. BROWNING IN FRONT

7TH ROYAL DUBLIN FUSILIERS: COLONEL DOWNING WITH OFFICERS AND
SERGEANTS OF "D" COMPANY

7TH ROYAL DUBLIN FUSILIERS: "D" COMPANY, No. 13 PLATOON

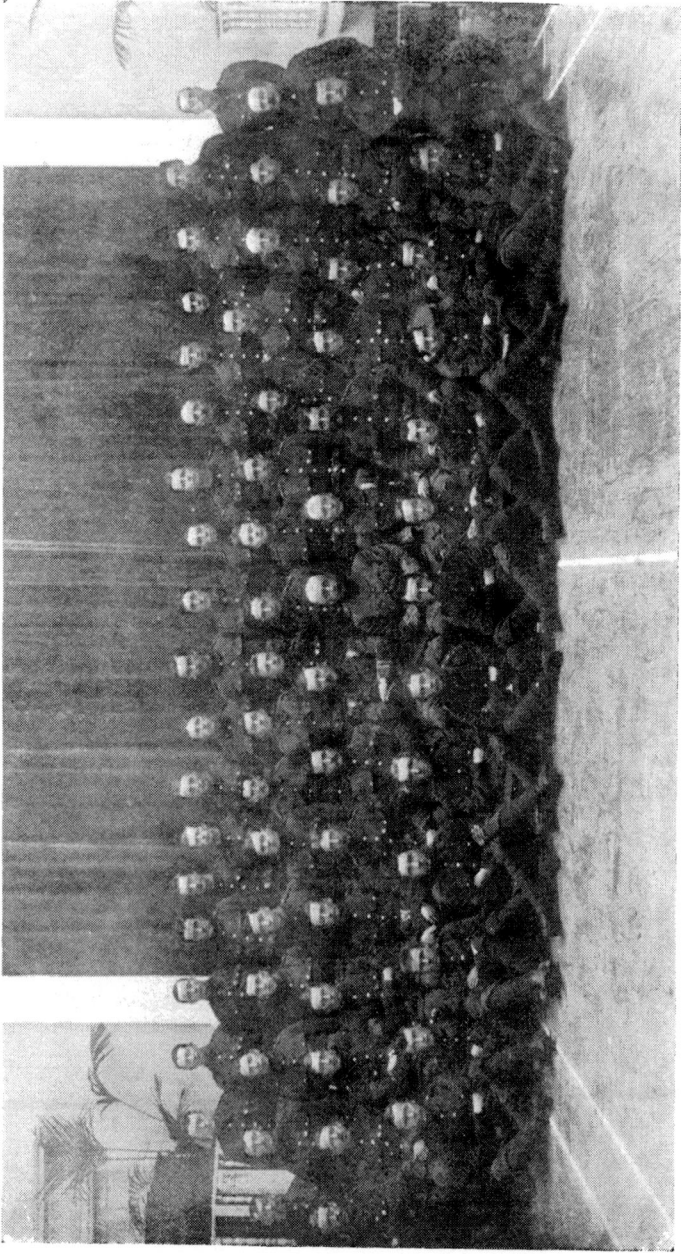

7TH ROYAL DUBLIN FUSILIERS: "D" COMPANY, No. 14 PLATOON

7TH ROYAL DUBLIN FUSILIERS: "D" COMPANY, No. 15 PLATOON

7TH ROYAL DUBLIN FUSILIERS: "D" COMPANY, No. 16 PLATOON

MR. F. H. BROWNING

PRESIDENT OF THE IRISH RUGBY FOOTBALL UNION 1914
AND COMMANDANT OF THE I.R.F.U. VOLUNTEERS

REV. FATHER MURPHY, C.F.

REV. CANON M'CLEAN, C.F.

" WHO'S WHO " OF THE PALS

SHORT BIOGRAPHICAL NOTES AND PHOTOGRAPHS OF THE
THREE HUNDRED PALS

ADAMS, HERBERT JAMES

Born at Dundalk. Son of F. J. Adams of same place. Educated at Institution, Dundalk. Clerk, Bank of Ireland. Wounded, Suvla, August 7, 1915. Invalided from Army, May 1916.

ALLEN, WILLIAM

Born at Donard, Co. Wicklow. Son of Anthony Allen of same place. Educated at Donard and Sligo Grammar School. Undergraduate Trinity College, Dublin. Gazetted Second Lieutenant 15th King's Liverpool Regiment, December 1915.

ALEXANDER, GEORGE GORDON

Born at Castledawson, Co. Derry. Son of the late T. J. Alexander, LL.D. (Senior Inspector, National Board of Education), Dublin. Educated at St. Luke's School, Cork. Was a member of Monkstown Football Club. Clerk in Provincial Bank of Ireland, Dublin.

ALMOND, CHARLES STOTT

Born at Wigan. Son of Frank Almond, Wigan. Educated at Wesleyan School, Wigan, and Wigan Grammar School. Second Division Clerk, Registry of Deeds Office, Dublin. Now Colour-Sergeant and stationed at Alexandria, Egypt.

ALEXANDER, PERCIVAL ALFRED

Born at Limerick. Son of James Alexander of that city. Educated at Villiers School, Limerick. Clerk in Provincial Bank of Ireland. Officially reported missing since August 16, 1915. Unofficially reported wounded, and probably prisoner of war.

ANDERSON, HUGH

Born at Donegal. Son of J. Anderson. Educated at Mountjoy School, Dublin, and played for their 1st xv, Rugby Football Seasons 1908-9 and 1909-10. Civil Servant. Gun-shot wounds chest, right arm, and left side, August 7, 1915. Dangerously ill August 15, and invalided September 15, 1915. Attached to 10th Royal Dublin Fusiliers from February to May 1916, and made Sergeant. Now in Cadet Corps, Curragh.

THE PALS AT SUVLA BAY

HERBERT JAMES ADAMS

WILLIAM ALLEN

GEORGE GORDON ALEXANDER

CHARLES STOTT ALMOND

PERCIVAL ALFRED ALEXANDER

HUGH ANDERSON

APPLEYARD, WALTER D'AUCIE

Born at Dublin. Son of William Appleyard, Dublin. Educated at High School, Dublin. Civil Servant, Irish Land Commission. Killed in action, August 16, 1915.

ARTHURS, GEORGE CHARLES

Born at Dublin. Son of G. W. Arthurs, Rathgar, Dublin. Educated at Wesley College, Dublin. Clerk in Chicago, U.S.A. Gun-shot wound, August 7, 1915. Invalided, October 10, 1915.

ARMSTRONG, CHARLES MARTYN

Born at Portadown. Son of Rev. Canon S. C. Armstrong, Kilrush, Co. Clare. Educated privately. Under-graduate, Trinity College, Dublin. Invalided, September 8, 1915. Gazetted Second Lieutenant 6th Royal Dublin Fusiliers, January 1916.

ATKINSON, JAMES M.

Born at Holywood, Co. Down. Son of Rev. A. H. Atkinson, now of Kilrush, Ferns. Educated at Campbell College, Belfast, and Trinity College, Dublin. Gazetted Second Lieutenant Army Service Corps, November 6, 1914.

ARMSTRONG, RICHARD

Born at Kilpatrick House, Co. Wicklow. Son of Richard Armstrong, B.L., King's Inns, Dublin. Educated at Wicklow Academy and Mountjoy School, Dublin. Civil Servant, Land Registry, Ireland. Suvla and Salonika.

ATKINSON, W. H.

Son of T. N. Atkinson, Dornden, Booterstown, Co. Dublin. Educated at Trinity College, Dublin. Member of Irish Bar, North-West Circuit. Invalided, August 28, 1915; rejoined, October 18, 1915. Sergeant, December 12, 1914. Commission, February 16, 1916, 7th Royal Dublin Fusiliers. Suvla, Balkans, Salonika.

THE PALS AT SUVLA BAY

WALTER D'AUCIE APPLEYARD

GEORGE CHARLES ARTHURS

CHARLES MARTYN ARMSTRONG

JAMES M. ATKINSON

RICHARD ARMSTRONG

W. H. ATKINSON

ATTRIDGE, JAMES CHARLES

Born at Skibbereen, Co. Cork. Son of Thomas Attridge, Mallow. Educated at Queen's College, Cork, and Royal College of Surgeons, Ireland. Medical Student. Dysentery, September 16, 1915. Invalided, October 7, 1915.

BALL, CHARLES FREDERICK

Born at Loughborough, Leicestershire. Son of Mr. Alfred Ball. Educated at Grammar School, Loughborough. Assistant-keeper, Royal Botanic Gardens, Dublin, and Editor of *Irish Gardening*. Married in December 1914, Alice, daughter of the late T. F. Lane, Dublin. Died of shrapnel wounds received the same day, at " Rest Camp, " Gallipoli, on September 13, 1915.

BAILEY, CHARLES

Born at Dublin. Son of Mr. A. Bailey of that city. Educated at High School and St. Andrew's College, Dublin. Clerk. Made Lance-Corporal, August 19, 1915. Invalided, suffering from dysentery, August 1915. Gazetted Second Lieutenant 7th Munsters, October 1915. Transferred to 10th Royal Dublin Fusiliers, January 1916, and is now Lieutenant and Adjutant of that Battalion.

BARBOUR, J.

Born at Londonderry. Son of Thomas Barbour. Educated at Model School, Londonderry. Commercial Traveller. Lance-Corporal, September 28, 1914. Transferred to " C " Company, October 31, 1914. Commission, December 1, 1914, 7th Royal Dublin Fusiliers. Attached Royal Irish Garrison Regiment. At Suvla. Now Transport Officer, Kingsbridge, Dublin.

BAKER, CECIL

Born at Dalkey, Co. Dublin. Son of the late H. F. Baker of same place. Educated at Presentation College, Kingstown, Co. Dublin, and Salesian School, Battersea, London.

BARRETT, EDWARD ROBERT

Born at Wicklow. Son of George W. Barrett, Rathgar, Dublin. Educated at Rathgar School and Rosse College, Dublin. Civil Servant, Custom House, Dublin.

JAMES CHARLES ATTRIDGE

CHARLES FREDERICK BALL

CHARLES BAILEY

J. BARBOUR

CECIL BAKER

EDWARD ROBERT BARRETT

BAYLEY, JASPER UNIACKE

Born at Killough Castle, Thurles. Son of E. C. Bayley, of Killough Castle, Thurles, and Rathmines, Dublin. Educated at High School and Wesley College, Dublin.

BLACK, T. S. C.

Son of Wm. Black, J.P., of Bally-leck, Co. Monaghan. Student. Promoted Lance-Corporal, September 28, 1914; Corporal, January 1, 1915; Sergeant, March 12, 1915. Wounded, Suvla, August 9, 1915. Died of wounds in Alexandria, September 25, 1915.

BELL, CHARLES FREDERICK JAMES

Born at Kilkenny. Son of the late James Bell, of Armagh. Educated at Royal School, Armagh. Junior Examiner, National Health Insurance Commission, Ireland. Killed in action, August 16, 1915.

BLACKMORE, INSLEY

Born at Shrewsbury. Son of J. Blackmore. Educated at Barry Council and County Schools. Engineer Surveyor, Board of Trade, Dublin. Gazetted Engineer Lieutenant Royal Navy, July 1916. One of the reserves left at Mudros who rejoined Battalion, August 16, 1915.

BIBLE, G. R.

Son of Henry Bible, Dublin. Educated at St. Andrew's College and Rathmines College, Dublin. Clerk. Commission, 9th Royal Sussex Regiment, November 1914. Killed in Battle of Somme, July 1, 1916, at Contalmaison.

BLACKMORE, PERCY B.

Born at Barry, Glamorganshire. Brother of I. Blackmore. Educated at Barry Council and County Schools. Insurance Clerk. One of the reserves left at Mudros who rejoined Battalion, August 16, 1915.

JASPER UNIACKE BAYLEY

T. S. C. BLACK

CHARLES FREDERICK JAMES BELL

INSLEY BLACKMORE

G. R. BIBLE

PERCY B. BLACKMORE

BLOUNT, ALFRED M.

Born at Holywood, Co. Down. Son of Naval Lieutenant C. N. Blount. Educated at Methodist College, Belfast. Founder, Library for British residents at Buenos Ayres. Returned home to join Army.

BOURKE, ROBERT S.

Born at Dublin. Brother of E. C. Bourke. Educated at Diocesan School, Dublin. Made Lance-Corporal, January 1915; Corporal, February 1915, and transferred from " D " to " A " Company; Lance-Sergeant, June 1915. Gun-shot wound in left heel and toe, August 1915. Invalided, September 1915. Gazetted Second-Lieutenant 2nd Royal Dublin Fusiliers, June 1916.

BOURKE, EDMUND C.

Born at Dublin. Son of H. Bourke. Educated at Diocesan School, Dublin. Accountant.

BOURKE, THOMAS L.

Born at Dublin. Brother of E. C. and R. S. Bourke. Educated at Diocesan School, Dublin. Member 1st City Dublin Cadets. Pioneer, Gun-shot wound right forearm, August 7, 1915. Since rejoined Battalion at Salonika.

BOURKE, EDWARD P.

Born at Kingstown, Co. Dublin. Son of Edward Bourke, of Ballsbridge, Dublin. Educated at Clongowes Wood College. Insurance Clerk. Developed pneumonia, August 6, 1915. Invalided, September 8, 1915. At present attached to 10th Battalion Royal Dublin Fusiliers.

BOYD, FREDERICK ENNIS

Born at Dublin. Son of J. Ennis Boyd of that city. Educated at Rathgar Boys' School. Book-keeper, The Union Assurance Society, Limited, Dublin.

THE PALS AT SUVLA BAY

ALFRED M. BLOUNT

ROBERT S. BOURKE

EDMUND C. BOURKE

THOMAS L. BOURKE

EDWARD P. BOURKE

FREDERICK ENNIS BOYD

BOYD, HARRY

Born at Blackrock, Co. Dublin. Son of Wm. H. Boyd, of Stillorgan, Co. Dublin. Educated at Monkstown Park, Co. Dublin, and Dean Close School, Cheltenham. In business with his father, who is a member of the firm of Boileau and Boyd, Dublin.

BRETT, JASPER THOMAS

Born at Kingstown, Co. Dublin. Son of Wm. Jasper Brett of same place. Educated at Monkstown Park School and Royal School, Armagh. Apprenticed to his father, W. J. Brett, Solicitor. Member of Monkstown Rugby Football Club, and obtained his International Cap for Rugby Football Season 1913–14, and played in Sir Stanley Cochrane's Cricket Team. Transferred to Machine-Gun Section, " B " Company, 7th Royal Dublin Fusiliers, December 1914. Gazetted Second Lieutenant 7th Royal Dublin Fusiliers, September 5, 1915.

BOYD, JOHN

Born at Cavan. Son of the late John Boyd, Provincial Bank, Cavan. Educated at Masonic Boys' School, Dublin. Second Division Clerk, Department of Agriculture, Dublin. Member of Clontarf Football and Cricket Clubs and Finglas Golf Club. Transferred from 11th Hussars to " D " Company, 7th Royal Dublin Fusiliers, January 1915. Missing since August 16, 1915.

BRIDGE, WILLIAM PUREFOY

Born at Barnagree, Roscrea, Co. Tipperary. Son of J. Smith Bridge, of Donnybrook, Dublin. Educated at Strangway's School and Trinity College, Dublin. Solicitor. Gun-shot wound in lung, August 7, 1915, of which he died, on H.M. *Alaunia*, on August 10, 1915, and was buried at sea the same day.

BOYD, WILLIAM ST. CLAIR

Born at Dublin. Son of J. St. Clair Boyd, of Ranelagh, Dublin. Educated at Diocesan School, Molesworth Street, Dublin. Commercial Traveller. Member of Bective Rangers Rugby Football Club. Missing since bayonet charge, August 16, 1915.

BRIGHT, HAROLD S.

Born at Kingstown, Co. Dublin. Son of Dr. W. Bright, now of Whitechurch, Co. Dublin. Educated at Ranelagh School, Athlone. First-class Clerk, Guinness's Brewery. Gazetted Second Lieutenant 7th Royal Munster Fusiliers, September 1915. Mentioned in dispatches for gallantry, and awarded Military Cross, June 1916.

HARRY BOYD

JASPER THOMAS BRETT

JOHN BOYD

WILLIAM PUREFOY BRIDGE

WILLIAM ST. CLAIR BOYD

HAROLD S. BRIGHT

165

BROOKS, HAROLD B. J.

Born at Killarney, Co. Kerry. Son of late T. J. Brooks. Educated at St. Vincent's College, Castleknock, Co. Dublin. Assistant Purser, Allen Line. Gun-shot wounds right arm and shoulder, August 7, 1915, of which he died, in Field Ambulance 35 (Gallipoli), on August 8, 1915.

BULL, JOHN

Born at Dundrum, Co. Tipperary. Son of the late William Bull, Ballymahon, Co. Longford. Educated at Masonic Boys' School, Dublin. Solicitor's Clerk. Gazetted Second-Lieutenant Royal Inniskilling Fusiliers, September 1915.

BROWN, JOHN FREDERIC WILLIAM

Born at Dundalk. Son of Lieutenant-Colonel A. E. Brown, Shrewsbury. Educated at Bancroft School, Woodford, Essex. Chief Clerk, Accountant-General's Office, Bank of Ireland, Dublin. Gun-shot wound, August 16, 1916 (slight). Invalided to Malta with low fever, early 1916. Now Lance-Corporal, doing garrison duty at Malta.

BURNS, ROBERT

Born at Booterstown, Co. Dublin. Son of Joseph Burns, of Blackrock, Co. Dublin. Educated at Christian Schools, Kingstown, Co. Dublin. Clerk in Land Registry, Dublin.

BRYCE, JAMES

Born at Milngavie, Glasgow. Son of James Bryce, Clontarf, Dublin. Educated at Howth Road and Skerry's College, Dublin. Clerk. Member of Clontarf Rugby Football Club.

BURNS, ROBERT H.

Born at Bandon, Co. Cork. Son of Robert H. Burns, of Provincial Bank, Cork. Educated at Cavendish Quay School, Bandon. Bank official.

THE PALS AT SUVLA BAY

HAROLD B. J. BROOKS

JOHN BULL

JOHN FREDERIC WILLIAM BROWN

ROBERT BURNS

JAMES BRYCE

ROBERT H. BURNS

BURROWES, A. E.

Son of S. J. Burrowes, Palmerston Road, Dublin. Educated at Merchant Taylors' School. Insurance employee. Promoted Lance-Corporal, December 1914; Sergeant, February 1915. Commission at Suvla Bay, September 14, 1915. Serbia and Salonika.

CAMPBELL, SAMUEL WILSON

Born near Ballyclare, Co. Antrim. Son of James Campbell of same place. Educated at Intermediate School, Ballyclare. Second Division Clerk, General Post Office, Dublin.

BUTLER, GEORGE VICTOR

Born at Dublin. Son of J. Marshall Butler, of Sutton, Co. Dublin. Educated at High School, Dublin. Stockbroker. Gazetted Second Lieutenant Army Service Corps, February 8, 1915, and Lieutenant, March 27, 1916.

CARPENTER, JOHN HENRY

Born at Barnes, Surrey. Son of Louis Carpenter. Educated at Fulham, London.

CALWELL, WM. M.

Born at Dublin. Son of J. Calwell, of Dublin. Educated at Rathmines. Clerk. Transferred to 3rd Royal Dublin Fusiliers, July 1915. Made Lance-Corporal, Corporal, and Bombing Sergeant. Gazetted Second Lieutenant 10th Royal Dublin Fusiliers, January 1916.

CASH, WALTER STAFFORD

Born at Birmingham. Son of Charles Cash of same place. Educated at King Edward's Grammar School, Birmingham. Commercial Traveller. Was one of those disembarked at Mudros, July 30, 1915, and rejoined Battalion at Suvla, August 16, 1915. Removed to Alexandria, suffering from varicose veins, September 11, 1915, and employed there as Clerk since October 1915.

A. E. BURROWES

SAMUEL WILSON CAMPBELL

GEORGE VICTOR BUTLER

JOHN HENRY CARPENTER

WM. M. CALWELL

WALTER STAFFORD CASH

M

CATHIE, DONALD COLIN

Born at Plymouth. Son of R. A. Cathie. Educated at Christ's Hospital, West Horsham, Surrey, and St. Andrew's College, Dublin. Pioneer. He was invalided with fever in August 1915, and rejoined Battalion in November 1915. He is now Lance-Corporal.

CLEMENTS, WILLIAM HARTE

Born near Hillsborough, Co. Down. Son of Rev. Dr. Andrew Clements. Educated at Anahilt School, Hillsborough. Bank Clerk. He acted as stretcher-bearer. Developed dysentery in August 1915, and was invalided to Alexandria. Rejoined in October 1915, and is stationed at Alexandria.

CLARKE, GEORGE A.

Born in Scotland. Son of A. Clarke, now of Dublin. Educated at Mountjoy School, Dublin. Insurance Clerk. One of the transport. Invalided to Malta, suffering from fever, June 1916.

CLARK, JAMES FREDERICK

Born at Dublin. Son of J. Clark. Educated at St. Andrew's College, Dublin. Clerk, G. S. and W. Railway, Ireland. Made Lance-Corporal, April 1915. One of the transport.

CLERY, WILLIAM J. O'F.

Born at Cork. Son of Richard W. Clery. Educated at Presentation College, Glasthule, Co. Dublin. Bank Clerk. He developed colitis in September 1915, and is now in " Rest Camp " at Cairo.

DONALD COLIN CATHIE

WILLIAM HARTE CLEMENTS

GEORGE A. CLARKE

JAMES FREDERICK CLARK

WILLIAM J. O'F. CLERY

COLDWELL, ERNEST GEORGE

Born at Dublin. Son of F. G. Coldwell, of Glenageary, Co. Dublin. Educated at Corrig School, Kingstown, Co. Dublin. Outfitter. Won the National Graceful Diving Championship at Highgate, London, in 1900. Was a member of Old Wesley and Lansdowne Football Clubs, and also of Bohemian Football Club.

COX, JOHN FRANCIS

Born at Strabane, Co. Tyrone. Son of Mr. Henry Cox (Senior Inspector, National Schools), Dublin. Educated at S.S.G. School and Trinity College, Dublin. Divinity Student. Member of Trinity 1st Cricket Team, and Captain of Lansdowne 2nd Rugby Football Team. Gazetted Second Lieutenant Royal Irish Fusiliers, September 14, 1915. Awarded Military Cross, 1916.

CONAN, FRANK

Born at Dublin. Son of Alexander Conan. Educated at Belvidere College, Dublin. Merchant Tailor. Was made a Corporal in September 1914, and gazetted Second Lieutenant in the Army Service Corps (Motor Transport) in October of the same year. At present holds the rank of Captain.

CRADDOCK, JAMES JOSEPH

Born at Rathmines, Dublin. Son of James Craddock of same place. Educated at Rathmines School. Motor Mechanic. At Suvla and Salonika.

CORRELL, WILLIAM J.

Born at Killiney, Co. Dublin. Son of J. Correll, of Dublin. Educated at St. Paul's School, Dublin. Made Lance-Corporal, April 1915. Gun-shot wound in right heel, August 7, 1915. Invalided to Alexandria, but is now Corporal with Battalion at Salonika.

CRANWILL, GUY BUTLER

Born at Monkstown, Co. Dublin. Son of Thomas B. Cranwill of same place. Educated at Monkstown Park School and King's Hospital, Dublin.

ERNEST GEORGE COLDWELL

JOHN FRANCIS COX

FRANK CONAN

JAMES JOSEPH CRADDOCK

WILLIAM J. CORRELL

GUY BUTLER CRANWILL

CRICHTON, ALEXANDER G.

Born at Dublin. Son of Mr. A. Crichton. Educated at St. Christopher's Preparatory School, Eastbourne ; Sherborne School, Dorset ; Aspatria Agricultural College, and Trinity College, Dublin. Engineer. Made Lance-Corporal, December 1914 ; Corporal, January 1915. Gazetted Second Lieutenant 7th Royal Dublin Fusiliers, April 1915. Missing, believed killed, August 16, 1915.

CUNNIAM, JOSEPH F.

Born at Dublin. Son of T. Cunniam. Educated at St. Thomas's College, Newbridge, Co. Kildare. Married, March 1915. Agent. Invalided, suffering from rheumatism, August 24, 1915. Gazetted Second Lieutenant Army Service Corps, October 1915, and now serving in France.

CROOKSHANK, ARTHUR CHICHESTER

Born at Dublin. Son of Chas. H. Crookshank, of Dundrum, Co. Dublin. Educated at Mr. Strangway's School and St. Columba's College, Dublin. Law Student, Trinity College, Dublin, and Solicitor's Apprentice. Captain of 1st xv Rugby Football, and winner of Ballinter Cup for All-round Sport, St. Columba's College. Sergeant, August 9, 1915. Recommended for D.C.M., and missing, August 16, 1915.

D'ALTON, MICHAEL J.

Born at Dublin. Son of M. D'Alton. Educated at Catholic University School, Dublin. Clerk, National Bank, Dublin. Member of Lansdowne Football and Killiney Golf Clubs. Made Lance-Corporal, September 1914, and Corporal following December ; Sergeant, January 1915. Gun-shot wounds right heel and left shoulder, August 10, 1915. Invalided home, October 1915.

CROOKSHANK, HENRY

Born at Dublin. Brother of Sergeant A. Crookshank. Educated at Mr. Strangway's School and St. Columba's College, Dublin. Engineering Student, Trinity College, Dublin. Transferred from " D " to " B " Company, 7th Royal Dublin Fusiliers (Machine-Gun Section), December 1914. Gun-shot wound, August 27, 1915. Invalided, September 1, 1915, and since gazetted Second Lieutenant in Royal Engineers.

DARCUS, FRANCIS EDWARD

Born at Dublin. Son of Solomon H. Darcus, of Kingstown, Co. Dublin. Educated privately. Clerk. Received a gun-shot wound on August 7, 1915, but rejoined in following October.

ALEXANDER G. CRICHTON

JOSEPH F. CUNNIAM

ARTHUR CHICHESTER CROOKSHANK

MICHAEL J. D'ALTON

HENRY CROOKSHANK

FRANCIS EDWARD DARCUS

DARLING, SYDNEY G.

Born at Clonmellon, Co. Westmeath. Son of the late John Darling of same place. Educated at Belfast. School Teacher. Member of Wanderers Football Club. Made Lance-Corporal in March 1915, and Transport Sergeant in following month.

DODD, FRANCIS J.

Born at Killorglin, Co. Kerry. Son of Dr. W. H. Dodd. Educated at Clongowes Wood College. Clerk in Provincial Bank of Ireland. Transferred from " D " Company to Machine-Gun Section of " B " Company in December 1914. Present rank : Sergeant.

DAVEY, REGINALD BARTON

Born at Cardiff. Son of Richard Davey of same place. Educated at Cardiff Municipal Secondary School. Inspector, National Insurance. Was one of the reserves who were left behind at Mudros and who rejoined Battalion at Suvla on August 16, 1915.

DONOVAN, JAMES W. C.

Born at Dalkey, Co. Dublin. Son of the late James Donovan of same place. Educated at Castleknock College. Member of Leinster Cricket Club and of Bohemian Football Club. Clerk in National Bank.

DAVIDSON, JAMES J. (JACK)

Born at Ballinasloe. Son of H. Davidson, Solicitor, of Ballinasloe. Educated at Mountpleasant School, Ballinasloe, and Grammar School, Galway. Solicitor's Apprentice. Wounded and missing since August 16, 1915.

DOUGLAS, ROBERT GRAHAM

Born at Portadown. Son of Joseph Douglas, now of Dalkey, Co. Dublin. Educated at The Grammar School, Kingstown, Co. Dublin, and The Abbey, Tipperary. Was one of the two elected to Commissions by their comrades in September 1914. Promoted Lieutenant May 1915. Invalided, suffering from colitis, August 25, 1915, but rejoined three days later. Again invalided with rheumatism in October 1915. Now Second-in-Command and Machine-Gun Instructor at School of Instruction, Cairo.

THE PALS AT SUVLA BAY

SYDNEY G. DARLING

FRANCIS J. DODD

REGINALD BARTON DAVEY

JAMES W. C. DONOVAN

JAMES J. (JACK) DAVIDSON

ROBERT GRAHAM DOUGLAS

DRUMMOND, DAVID

Born at Guildtown, Perthshire, N.B. Son of D. Drummond, now of New Scone, N.B. Civil Servant. Made Lance-Corporal, January 1915; Corporal, April 1915, and Sergeant, August 1915. Gun-shot wound in neck, August 16, 1915. *Rejoined Battalion at Salonika, October 1915. Killed at Salonika, 1916.*

DUDLEY, HENRY PEMBERTON

Born at Kinnitty, King's County. Son of Dr. Henry Dudley. Educated at Preston School, Abbeyleix, and at Portarlington. Clerk in Hong-Kong and Shanghai Bank. Promoted Lance-Corporal in March 1915. Received a gun-shot wound on August 7, 1915, and was invalided on the 14th of same month. Gazetted Second Lieutenant in the 3rd Leinsters, November 1915. Killed in action, France, September 3, 1916.

DOWSE, CHARLES EDWARD

Born at Monkstown, Co. Dublin. Son of Rev. Canon John C. Dowse of same place. Educated at Trent College, Derbyshire. He was promoted to be Lance-Corporal in January 1915, and Corporal in July. He was killed in action on August 16, 1915.

DUFFEY, ALFRED H.

Born in Dublin. Son of P. P. Duffey. Educated at St. Mary's College, Rathmines, and Clongowes Wood College. Clerk in Congested Districts Board.

DOWSE, HENRY HARVEY

Born at Glenageary, Co. Dublin. Elder brother of C. E. Dowse. Educated at Trent College, Derbyshire, and Trinity College, Dublin. Promoted Lance-Corporal September 17, 1914, and Corporal on the 28th of same month, and became Sergeant in March 1915. He received a severe gun-shot wound in chest on September 7, 1915, and was invalided the following month. In January 1916 he rejoined his regiment, but was gazetted Second Lieutenant in the Army Service Corps in February, and is now with his regiment in France.

EGAN, ARTHUR F.

Born at Blackrock, Co. Dublin. Son of the late A. Egan, of Dalkey. Educated at The Collegiate School, Blackrock. Electrical Engineer. Invalided, suffering from dysentery, August 22. Rejoined Battalion in October 1915.

THE PALS AT SUVLA BAY

DAVID DRUMMOND

HENRY PEMBERTON DUDLEY

CHARLES EDWARD DOWSE

ALFRED H. DUFFEY

HENRY HARVEY DOWSE

ARTHUR F. EGAN

ELKAN, H.

Lance-Corporal, March 12, 1915. Wounded, Suvla, August 7, 1915.

ENGLAND, ARTHUR JOHN

Born at Portadown. Son of W. J. England, now of Kilkenny. Educated at Drogheda, Kilkenny College, and Mountjoy School, Dublin. Clerk in Irish Lights Office, Dublin. Made Sergeant in March 1915. Gazetted Second Lieutenant 7th Royal Dublin Fusiliers, May 1916.

ELLIOTT, THOMAS C. M.

Born at Strabane. Son of J. Elliott of same place. Educated at Strabane Academy, Portora Royal School, and Trinity College, Dublin. Medical Student. Member of Portora and Trinity College Rugby Football Teams, and obtained his Inter-Provincial Cap for Rugby for Ulster. One of the Portora Team who won All-Ireland Shield for Rifle Shooting. Killed in action, August 16, 1915.

ENNIS, CHARLES F. K.

Born at Dublin. Son of C. Ennis. Educated at St. Mary's College, Rathmines, Dublin. Civil Servant. Made Lance-Corporal, August 16, 1915.

ELVERY, JOHN W.

Born at Dublin. Son of J. H. Elvery, of Bray, Co. Wicklow. Educated at Aravon, Bray. Secretary and Director, Messrs. Elvery and Co., Ltd., Dublin. Member of Delgany and Greystones Cricket Clubs, Bray Golf Club. Organist, Christ Church, Bray. Made Lance-Corporal September 28, 1914 ; Corporal, January 1915 ; Lance-Sergeant, August 9, 1915.

EVANS, ROBERT RITSON

Born at Dublin. Son of F. R. Evans of same city. Educated at Diocesan School, Dublin. Engineer. Received a gun-shot wound in back, August 29, 1915, and was invalided on October 27, 1915. Now attached to the 10th Battalion Royal Dublin Fusiliers.

THE PALS AT SUVLA BAY

H. ELKAN

ARTHUR JOHN ENGLAND

THOMAS C. M. ELLIOTT

CHARLES F. K. ENNIS

JOHN W. ELVERY

ROBERT RITSON EVANS

EWEN, ARCHIBALD MURRAY

Born at Aberdeen. Son of J. Ewen of same city. Educated at Robert Gordon's College, Aberdeen. Clerk in D.A.T.I. (Fisheries Branch). Member of Bohemian Football Club. Promoted Corporal, August 1915. Gazetted Second Lieutenant "A" Company, 7th Royal Dublin Fusiliers, September 1915.

FARRELLY, MICHAEL

Born at Dublin. Son of J. Farrelly of same city. Educated at Christian Brothers Schools, Dublin. Insurance Agent.

EXSHAW, ROLAND L.

Born at Dungannon. Son of T. C. Exshaw, now of Monaghan. Clerk. Transferred from "D" Company to Machine-Gun Section of "B" Company, February 1915. Promoted Sergeant in September 1915.

FAUSSET, V. H.

Third son of Rev. C. Fausset, Dublin. Wounded at Kizlar Dagh, August 16, 1915. Died of wounds on H.S. *Gloucester Castle* at Mudros, August 19, 1915.

FALKINER, FREDERICK E. B.

Born at Terenure, Dublin. Son of late Henry Baldwin Falkiner, Solicitor. Educated at St. Stephen's Green School, St. Columba's College, and Trinity College, Dublin. Solicitor's Apprentice. Sergeant Machine-Gun Section at Suvla, Serbia, and Salonika. Specially commended for saving the machine-guns in retreat from Serbia. Recommended for Commission, and now Cadet at Moor Park, Fermoy.

FIELD, SYDNEY H.

Born at Great Grimsby. Son of W. J. Field, now of Dublin. Educated at Epworth College, Rhyl, N. Wales, and Royal University, Ireland. Clerk, Atlas Insurance Company, Dublin. Gazetted Second Lieutenant 4th Royal Inniskillings, December 1915. Killed in France by gas-poisoning, August 9, 1916.

ARCHIBALD MURRAY EWEN

MICHAEL FARRELLY

ROLAND L. EXSHAW

V. H. FAUSSET

FREDERICK E. B. FALKINER

SYDNEY H. FIELD

FINDLATER, CHARLES A.

Born at Dublin. Son of John Findlater of same city. Educated at Royal School, Armagh ; High School and Trinity College, Dublin. Engineer. Gun-shot wound in left knee, August 21, 1915, and was invalided three days later. Corporal and attached to 10th Royal Dublin Fusiliers. Killed in France December 1916.

FITZGERALD, LANCELOT C.

Born at Assam. Son of G. R. FitzGerald. Educated at Strangway's School, Dublin. Engineer. Gazetted Second Lieutenant 5th Royal Irish Fusiliers, October 1914. Now Captain.

FINDLATER, HERBERT S.

Brother of Charles A. Findlater Educated at Strangway's School and Trinity College, Dublin. M.A. (T.C.D.). Solicitor. Promoted Lance-Corporal, July 1915. Wounded and missing since August 16, 1915.

FITZGIBBON, MICHAEL J.

Son of John FitzGibbon, M.P., Castlerea, Co. Roscommon. Educated at Clongowes Wood College. Law Student. Commission in " D " Company, September 1914. Gazetted Captain, March 16, 1915. At Suvla Bay. Killed at Kizlar Dagh, August 16, 1915.

FISHER, CLARENCE G. C.

Born at Howden, Yorkshire. Son of the late Dr. Fisher, of Bournemouth. Educated at Hailey School, Bournemouth, and Forest School, Essex. First-class Clerk, Guinness's Brewery. Was one of the reserves left at Mudros who rejoined Battalion at Suvla, August 16, 1915.

FORBES, ALFRED

Born at Louisburgh, Co. Mayo. Son of Rev. J. Forbes, of Louisburgh, Co. Mayo. Educated at Ranelagh School, Athlone ; Mountjoy School and Trinity College, Dublin. Made Corporal, August 1915.

CHARLES A. FINDLATER

LANCELOT C. FITZGERALD

HERBERT S. FINDLATER

MICHAEL J. FITZGIBBON

CLARENCE G. C. FISHER

ALFRED FORBES

FORD, REGINALD G. J.

Born at Exeter. Son of J. Ford, of Exeter. Educated at St. Paul's School and Marlborough Street Training College, Dublin. Schoolmaster. Gun-shot wound and fracture left elbow, August 16, 1915. Invalided home, September 1915, and discharged from service as medically unfit, June 1916.

FRAZER, DAVID M.

Born at Dublin. Son of D. Frazer, now of Dalkey, Co. Dublin. Educated at High School, Dublin. First-class Clerk, Guinness's Brewery. Transferred from " D " Company to Machine-Gun Section " B " Company, December 1914, and acted as range-finder. Gazetted Second Lieutenant Connaught Rangers, September 1915. Now invalided.

FREEMAN, GEOFFREY J.

Born at Monkstown, Co. Dublin. Son of D. Freeman, of Dublin. Educated at Clongowes Wood College and in Austrian Tyrol. Stockbroker.

GALLAGHER, GEORGE M.

Born at Dublin. Son of J. Gallagher, of Kingstown, Co. Dublin. Educated at Christian Brothers Schools, Dublin. Clerk. Made Corporal. Transferred from " C " Company to " D " Company in February 1915. Received gun-shot wound in left foot, August 22, 1915, and was invalided two days later. Now attached to 10th Battalion Royal Dublin Fusiliers.

GARNHAM, JOHN H.

Born in London. Son of H. Garnham, of Aberdeen. Educated at Marylebone Higher Grade School, London. Waiter. Transferred to 3rd Royal Dublin Fusiliers in July 1915.

GIBSON, HENRY W.

Born at Dublin. Son of A. H. Gibson, of Ranelagh, Dublin. Educated at Wesley College, Dublin. Works Manager, Messrs. Bailey, Son, and Gibson. One of the reserves left at Mudros who rejoined Battalion, August 16, 1915. Gun-shot wound in right shoulder, August 29, 1915, and invalided three days later.

THE PALS AT SUVLA BAY

REGINALD G. J. FORD

GEORGE M. GALLAGHER

DAVID M. FRAZER

JOHN H. GARNHAM

GEOFFREY J. FREEMAN

HENRY W. GIBSON

GICK, THOMAS M.

Born at Dublin. Son of C. Hemsley Gick, of Sandymount, Co. Dublin. Educated at Grammar School, Kingstown. Clerk, G.S.W. Railway. Gazetted Second Lieutenant 14th Battalion Manchester Regiment, December 1914, but is attached to 14th King's Liverpool Regiment. At Salonika.

GRAY, EDWARD R.

Born at Sandymount, Co. Dublin. Son of W. Gray. Educated at High School, Dublin. Clerk, Bank of Ireland. Made Lance Corporal in February 1915. Invalided, otorrhœa, September 1915. Rejoined two days later, but was again invalided, suffering from jaundice, in October, and rejoined Battalion in December 1915.

GOURLAY, WILLIAM N.

Born at Dublin. Son of R. Gourlay of same city. Educated at Mountjoy School, Dublin. Second Division Clerk, D.A.T.I. (Fisheries Branch).

GRAY, WILLIAM V.

Born at Swansea. Son of A. Gray, now of Dublin. Educated at Drumcondra School. Clerk. Invalided, suffering from scarlet fever, August 1915.

GRANT, JOHN

Born at Belfast. Son of S. Grant, of Ballygowan, Belfast. Educated at Belfast Mercantile College. Clerk, G.N. Railway (Ireland). Made Corporal in March 1915. Compound fracture of thigh from gun-shot wound, August 9, 1915. Invalided, November 1915.

GREGOR, W. J.

Private. Wounded, Suvla, September 14, 1915. Invalided, November 19, 1915.

THE PALS AT SUVLA BAY

THOMAS M. GICK

EDWARD R. GRAY

WILLIAM N. GOURLAY

WILLIAM V. GRAY

JOHN GRANT

W. J. GREGOR

GUEST, ALLEN

Born at Cloghjordan, Co. Tipperary. Son of A. Guest. Married, 1895. Made Company Sergeant-Major, September 16, 1914, and Regimental Sergeant-Major in July 1915. Awarded D.C. Medal with Clasp. Commission in 7th Royal Dublin Fusiliers, September 1916.

GUY, JOHN W.

Born at Sunday's Well, Cork. Son of F. B. Guy, of Cork. Educated at Grammar School and Christian Brothers College, Cork. Myalgia, October 25, 1915. Rejoined Battalion in December 1915, and is now at Salonika.

GUNNING, FRANK D.

Born at Enniskillen. Son of S. Gunning of same place. Educated at Portora Royal School. Clerk, Bank of Ireland. Dysentery, August 19, 1915, and invalided four days later. Gazetted Second Lieutenant 6th Inniskillings, December 1915. Now serving in France.

GUNNING, GEORGE C.

Brother of F. D. Gunning. Educated at Portora Royal School. Clerk, Belfast Bank. Invalided, suffering from jaundice, November 1915.

HAMILTON, ERNEST J.

Born at Portrush, Co. Antrim. Son of the late H. M. Hamilton, of Portrush. Educated at Academical Institution, Coleraine, and Trinity College, Dublin. Medical Student, Trinity College, Dublin. Made Lance-Corporal, September 1914 ; Corporal, October 1914. Gazetted Second Lieutenant 7th Royal Dublin Fusiliers, December 1914. Invalided, suffering from dysentery, August 24, 1915. Promoted Captain for services on field, August 1915.

THE PALS AT SUVLA BAY

ALLEN GUEST

JOHN W. GUY

FRANK D. GUNNING

GEORGE C. GUNNING

ERNEST J. HAMILTON

HARDING, SIDNEY W.

Born at Dublin. Son of E. Harding. Educated at Diocesan School, Dublin. Insurance Clerk. Gun-shot wound in right arm, and enteric, August 9, 1915. Invalided, October 25, 1915, and now attached to 10th Battalion Royal Dublin Fusiliers.

HARPER, F. LEITCH

Born at Belfast. Son of the late J. Harper of that city. Educated at Antrim Road School and Sargent's College, Belfast. Made Lance-Corporal, August 10, 1915. Served at Suvla, Serbia, Salonika. Subsequently Company Quartermaster-Sergeant 10th Royal Dublin Fusiliers. Killed in France, October 1916.

HARE, EDWARD H.

Born at Dublin. Son of Rev. H. Hare, of Dublin. Educated at Mountjoy School, Dublin. Made Corporal at Suvla Bay. Gun-shot wound in leg, August 7, 1915, but rejoined Battalion on 30th of same month.

HARVEY, CHARLES DACRE

Born at Athboy, Co. Meath. Son of T. A. Harvey. Educated at St. Oswald's College, Ellesmere. Associate in Arts, University of Oxford. Clerk, Bank of Ireland. Made Sergeant, October 1914. Gazetted Second Lieutenant 7th Royal Dublin Fusiliers, December 1914. Shrapnel wound in right shoulder, August 7, 1915, but has since rejoined Battalion.

HARE, GEORGE

Brother of E. H. Hare. Educated at Mountjoy School, Dublin. Civil Servant. Made Sergeant in September 1914. Gazetted Second Lieutenant 7th Royal Dublin Fusiliers, September 1915, and has since been promoted Captain.

HASSETT, E.

Colour-Sergeant " D " Company. Joined Army, December 20, 1879. Served with Royal Dublin Fusiliers in India and South African War. Pensioner Messenger, Irish Land Commission. Rejoined, September 1914, as Instructor. Posted to " D " Company, 7th Royal Dublin Fusiliers, at Curragh. Transferred to Sittingbourne to 4th Battalion, to which he is still attached.

THE PALS AT SUVLA BAY

SIDNEY W. HARDING

F. LEITCH HARPER

EDWARD H. HARE

CHARLES DACRE HARVEY

GEORGE HARE

E. HASSETT

193

HASSETT, JOHN M.

Colour-Sergeant. Nephew of Colour-Sergeant E. Hassett. Also Instructor to " D " Company.

HENNESSY, ALEXANDER L.

Born at Dublin. Son of S. M. Hennessy, of Kilmainham, Dublin. Educated at St. James's School, Dublin. Clerk, Jameson's Distillery. Transferred from " D " to " A " Company in March 1915.

HEATLEY, EDWARD N.

Born at Bray, Co. Wicklow. Son of R. Heatley. Educated at St. Paul's School, Bray. Builder's Foreman. Invalided, suffering from nervous exhaustion, August 24, 1915, but rejoined three days later. Again invalided, with jaundice, in November 1915.

HENRY, ARTHUR R.

Son of Major H. Henry, of Firmont, Sallins. Co. Kildare. Educated at Haileybury College. Acted as Orderly to Brigadier-General Nicol from Suvla landing until he was promoted Quartermaster-Sergeant. Invalided, suffering from enteric, in September 1915. Gazetted Second Lieutenant 3rd Battalion Royal Dublin Fusiliers, January 1916.

HENDERSON, JOHN S.

Born at Airdrie, Scotland. Son of M. Henderson, of Airdrie. Educated at Higher Grade School, Airdrie, and Skerry's College, Glasgow. Civil Servant. Made Lance-Corporal, December 1914 ; Corporal, January 1915, and Sergeant, February 1915, when he was transferred from " D " to " A " Company. Gun-shot wound left hand, right shoulder, and eye, and typhoid fever, August 16, 1915. Invalided home, October 1915. Now Company Sergeant-Major in 10th Royal Dublin Fusiliers.

HENRY, CHARLES LENNOX

Son of J. Henry, B.L., Dublin. Corporal. Suvla, Balkans, Salonika. Transferred to Cadet Corps, Fermoy, July 1916.

THE PALS AT SUVLA BAY

JOHN M. HASSETT

ALEXANDER L. HENNESSY

EDWARD N. HEATLEY

ARTHUR R. HENRY

JOHN S. HENDERSON

CHARLES LENNOX HENRY

HICKEY, EUGENE F.

Born at Cork. Son of E. Hickey. Educated at ChristianBrothers Schools, Cork. Member of Cork County Rugby Football, Shandon Boat and Wanderers Swimming Clubs. Made Lance-Corporal, September 1914, and Sergeant, August 16, 1915. Invalided, suffering from rheumatism and dysentery, November 1915. Now attached to 10th Royal Dublin Fusiliers.

HICKMAN, THOMAS O'B.

Brother of N. W. G. and Poole H. Hickman. Educated at The Abbey, Tipperary. Employed in Railway and Telegraphic Services in South America. One of the reserves left at Mudros who rejoined the Battalion at Suvla, August 16, 1915. Made Lieutenant 7th Royal Dublin Fusiliers, September 1915.

HICKMAN, NORMAN W. G.

Born at Kilmore, Knock, Co. Clare. Son of F. W. G. Hickman. Educated at Rosscaberry, Co. Cork, and The Abbey, Tipperary. Clerk, Provincial Bank of Ireland. Made Lance-Corporal in March 1915.

HILL, CHARLES L.

Born at Downpatrick. Son of H. Purdon Hill, now of Blackrock, Co. Dublin. Educated at Monkstown Park and Rossall, Fleetwood. Clerk, Guinness's Brewery. Gazetted Second Lieutenant Army Service Corps, November 1914.

HICKMAN, POOLE H.

Brother of N. W. G. Hickman. Educated at The Abbey, Tipperary, and Trinity College, Dublin. B.A. (Trinity College, Dublin). Barrister on Munster Circuit. Gazetted Second Lieutenant 7th Royal Dublin Fusiliers, September 22, 1914. Made Captain, January 7, 1915, and from that date was Officer Commanding " D " Company. Killed in leading bayonet charge, August 16, 1915.

HOLLAND, LEO

Born at Roorkee, India. Son of P. Holland, now of Dublin. Educated at Army and Christian Brothers Schools. Civil Servant. Gun-shot wound in left arm and cheek, and injuries to right eye, August 16, 1915. Invalided, September 1915, and now Corporal attached to 10th Royal Dublin Fusiliers.

THE PALS AT SUVLA BAY

EUGENE F. HICKEY

THOMAS O'B. HICKMAN

NORMAN W. G. HICKMAN

CHARLES L. HILL

POOLE H. HICKMAN

LEO HOLLAND

HONEYMAN, WALTER B.

Born at Kirkcaldy. Son of the late A. P. Honeyman, Solicitor, Blackrock, Co. Dublin. Actor. Shrapnel wound, August 16, 1915. Now Lance-Corporal and attached to " C " Company, 7th Royal Dublin Fusiliers.

HUGHES, THOMAS

Born in Dublin. Son of W. J. Hughes, of Malahide, Co. Dublin. Educated at St. Stephen's Green School and Trinity College, Dublin. B.A., B.L. (Trinity College, Dublin). Gazetted Second Lieutenant 6th Connaught Rangers, September 1914.

HORNER, GORDON S.

Born at Killiney, Co. Dublin. Son of J. W. Horner. Educated at Killiney School. Insurance Clerk. Invalided, suffering from dysentery, August 22, 1915. Rejoined Battalion in October 1915.

ISAAC, DAVID H.

Born at Dublin. Son of H. Isaac. Educated at Kildare Place School and privately. Librarian. Invalided from Battalion in June 1915, and discharged from Service as medically unfit, October 1915.

HOWDEN, FRANCIS W.

Born at Longford. Son of J. Howden, of Longford. Educated at Ranelagh School, Athlone. Clerk, City of Dublin Steam Packet Company. Invalided, suffering from enteric, August 22, 1915, but rejoined following week.

JACKSON, W.

Born at Dublin, son of Thomas Jackson. Educated at St. Catherine's Schools. Factory foreman. Promoted Co.Q.M.S. at Salonika. Served at Suvla, Serbia, etc.

WALTER B. HONEYMAN

THOMAS HUGHES

GORDON S. HORNER

DAVID H. ISAAC

FRANCIS W. HOWDEN

W. JACKSON

JEEVES, CHARLES A. V.

Born at Exeter. Son of Anthony Jeeves. Educated at Hele's School, Exeter, and privately. Civil Servant. Acted as stretcher-bearer. Was made Lance-Corporal, August 1915. Wounded in retreat from Serbia, December 1915.

JENKINS, THOMAS R.

Born at Oldcastle, Co. Meath. Son of T. F. Jenkins, of Oldcastle. Clerk, Northern Banking Company.

JEFFRESON, VICTOR

Born at Belfast. Son of E. Jeffreson, now of Dublin. Educated at Wesley College, Dublin. Clerk, Secretary's Department, Guinness's Brewery. Killed in action, August 23, 1915.

JENKINS, CUTHBERT E.

Born at Dublin. Son of H. Jenkins, of Dublin. Educated at Mountjoy School and Trinity College, Dublin. Member of Neptune Rowing Club and Clontarf Rugby Football Club. Transferred from " D " to " B " Company (Machine-Gun Section), April 1915. Gun-shot wound in head, August 16, 1915. Invalided, September 1915. Gazetted Second Lieutenant 10th Royal Dublin Fusiliers, July 1916.

JORDAN, CHARLES H.

Born at Dublin. Son of W. Jordan of same city. Educated at St. Patrick's Cathedral School. Engineer. In Transport Service.

CHARLES A. V. JEEVES

THOMAS R. JENKINS

VICTOR JEFFRESON

CUTHBERT E. JENKINS

CHARLES H. JORDAN

JOY, FREDERICK C. P.

Born at Banbridge, Co. Down. Son of R. Joy. Educated at Highgate School, London, and Trinity College, Dublin. B.A., Trinity College, Dublin. Captain, University Harriers, 1912. Chartered Accountant. Gazetted Second Lieutenant 3rd Royal Irish Rifles, September 1914. Promoted Lieutenant, June 1915, but killed in action at Hooge, France, a few days afterwards.

KARNEY, GEORGE WOLFE

Born at Edinburgh. Brother of D. N. Karney. Educated at John Ivory School, New Ross, and at Cork. Member of Barrow Boat Club. International Hockey Player, 1914. Made Lance-Corporal, August 10, 1915. Missing since August 16, 1915.

JULIAN, ERNEST L.

Born at Dublin. Son of J. Julian, of Dublin. Educated at Strangway's School, Dublin; Charterhouse and Trinity College, Dublin. Barrister. Reid Professor of Law, Trinity College, Dublin. Elected to Commission by members of "D" Company, September 1914. Gazetted Lieutenant, October 1914. Gun-shot wound back, August 7, 1915, and died of wound on Hospital Ship *Valdivia* on following day. Buried at sea.

KAVANAGH, HENRY A.

Born at Merrion, Co. Dublin. Son of W. Kavanagh. Educated at Diocesan School, Molesworth Street, Dublin. Solicitor's Clerk. Made Lance-Corporal, August 16, 1915. Killed in action in Balkans, September 23, 1916.

KARNEY, DAVID N.

Born at Edinburgh. Son of J. Karney, now of Dublin. Educated at John Ivory School, New Ross, and at Cork. Clerk in Bank of Ireland.

KEATING, JAMES J.

Born at Wexford. Son of D. Keating, of Ardara, Wexford. Educated at Clongowes Wood College. Invalided, suffering from jaundice, November 1915, but has since rejoined and is now attached to No. 6 Armoured Motor Battery, Salonika.

THE PALS AT SUVLA BAY

FREDERICK C. P. JOY

GEORGE WOLFE KARNEY

ERNEST L. JULIAN

HENRY A. KAVANAGH

DAVID N. KARNEY

JAMES J. KEATING

KEE, WILLIAM

Born at Meenagrove, Co. Donegal. Son of T. Kee. Educated at Mountjoy School and Trinity College, Dublin. Divinity Student. Made Sergeant, September 1914 ; Company Sergeant-Major, July 1915. Gazetted Second Lieutenant 7th Royal Dublin Fusiliers and Officer Commanding " D " Company, September 1915. Suvla, Serbia. Wounded, Salonika, October 1916. Mentioned in dispatches and awarded M.C.

KENT, ALBERT VICTOR

Born in Dublin. Son of J. Kent. Educated at St. Paul's Schools, Dublin. Made Lance-Corporal, May 1915. Stretcher-bearer. Gun-shot wound, August 9, 1915. Invalided five days later. Gazetted Second-Lieutenant 5th Connaught Rangers, January 1916.

KEESHAM, MAURICE

Born at Cork. Son of J. Keesham, of Cork. Educated at Presentation College, Cork. Member of Dolphin Rugby Football and Swimming and Shandon Boat Clubs. Transferred from " D " to " B " Company (Machine-Gun Section), April 1915. Gun-shot wound left leg, August 7, 1915, but rejoined Battalion at end of same month.

KELLER, CECIL CLAUDE

Born at New Jersey, U.S.A. Son of J. Keller, now of Dublin. Educated at Castleknock College and Marino, Clontarf. Apprentice, Mercantile Marine. Officially reported " missing " since August 16, 1915 ; unofficially reported " killed " on that date.

KERR, DAVID

Born at Carrickfergus, Co. Antrim. Son of D. Kerr of same place. Educated at Royal Academical Institution, Belfast. Second Division Clerk, Irish Land Commission. Gun-shot wound in left arm, August 7, 1915. Rejoined Battalion, October 14, 1915.

THE PALS AT SUVLA BAY

WILLIAM KEE

ALBERT VICTOR KENT

MAURICE KEESHAM

CECIL CLAUDE KELLER

DAVID KERR

KING, ALEXANDER W.

Born at Clontarf, Co. Dublin. Son of W. King, of Clontarf. Educated at St. Andrew's College. Married in 1911, one child. Clerk, Canadian Northern Railway. Held Squadron Championship of Leinster for 1901, 1902, and 1903, for swimming.

LEA, ALBERT VICTOR

Born at Burton-on-Trent. Son of Rev. W. Lea, now of Edgeworthstown, Co. Longford. Educated at Dr. Benson's School, Rathmines, Dublin, and Campbell College, Belfast. Clerk, Irish Land Commission. Gun-shot wound, August 9, 1915. Invalided, August 14, 1915, and now Corporal, attached to 10th Royal Dublin Fusiliers.

LAIRD, FRANCIS M.

Born at Dublin. Son of Rev. Caleb Laird. Educated at Wesley College, Dublin, and Dublin University. Civil Servant. Married, December 1915. Gun-shot wound in back, August 9, 1915; invalided on 26th of same month. Commissioned in 11th Royal Dublin Fusiliers, November 1916.

LECKY, HUGH

Born at Portrush. Son of H. Lecky. Educated at Clifton College, Bristol, and Trinity College, Dublin. M.A. (Trinity College, Dublin). Gazetted Second Lieutenant " D " Company. 7th Royal Dublin Fusiliers, March 1915. Promoted Lieutenant, August 15, 1915. Invalided, suffering from dysentery, August 1915. Now attached to 10th Royal Dublin Fusiliers.

LATIMER, HUGH G.

Born at Dublin. Son of J. Latimer, of Dublin. Clerk, Bank of Ireland. Invalided home, suffering from dysentery and sprained knee, in September 1915. Was attached to 10th Royal Dublin Fusiliers, but has now been discharged as " permanently medically unfit."

LEE, CHARLES G.

Private. High Street, Tullamore.

THE PALS AT SUVLA BAY

ALEXANDER W. KING

ALBERT VICTOR LEA

FRANCIS M. LAIRD

HUGH LECKY

HUGH G. LATIMER

CHARLES G. LEE

LEVIS, GEORGE J. F.

Born at Cootehill, Co. Cavan. Son of G. Levis. Educated at Drogheda Grammar School and Trinity College, Dublin. Medical Student. Gazetted Second Lieutenant Leinster Regiment, December 1914. Killed at St. Eloi, November 1915.

McALLEN, HAMILTON

Born at Ballymoney. Son of H. McAllen. Educated at Ballymoney Model and Intermediate Schools, Coleraine Academy, and Larne Grammar School. Clerk, Ulster Bank. Promoted Sergeant.

LITTLE, JOSEPH W.

Born at Castlegarron, Sligo. Son of S. Little, of Sligo. Educated at Sligo Intermediate School and Wesley College, Dublin. Civil Servant. Made Lance-Corporal, June 1915. Gun-shot wound in left knee, August 22, 1915. Died of septic poisoning, September 17, 1915.

McCARTHY, JAMES P.

Born at Listowel, Co. Kerry. Son of the late R. Hillgrove McCarthy. Educated at Bishop Foy High School, Waterford, and Skerry's College, Dublin. Clerk, Royal Bank of Ireland, Dublin.

LOOKER, ARTHUR N.

Born at Norwich. Son of F. Looker, now of Hale, Cheshire. Educated at Collegiate School, Rochdale. Inspector, Insurance (London, Liverpool, and Globe Company). Member of Cheshire Yeomanry; first-class shot. Killed in action, August 16, 1915.

McCARTHY, LESLIE

Born at Listowel, Co. Kerry. Brother of James P. McCarthy. Educated at Wesley College, Dublin, and at Cheltenham. Engaged in farming.

THE PALS AT SUVLA BAY

GEORGE J. F. LEVIS

HAMILTON McALLEN

JOSEPH W. LITTLE

JAMES P. McCARTHY

ARTHUR N. LOOKER

LESLIE McCARTHY

McCARTHY, WILLIAM T.

Born at Killarney, Co. Kerry. Son of W. P. T. McCarthy. Educated at Jeffers Institute, Tralee, and Clongowes Wood College. Solicitor's Apprentice.

McCULLAGH, ROBERT R.

Born at Dublin. Son of H. S. McCullagh, of Rathmines, Dublin. Educated by Dr. Robinson, Dublin. One of the reserves left behind at Mudros, who rejoined Battalion, August 16, 1915.

McCLELLAND, WILLIAM

Born at Dublin. Son of J. McClelland, of Dublin. Educated at Christ Church Cathedral Grammar School. Accountant. Member of Railway and Steam Packet Athletic Union, and Clonliffe Harriers. Won the Quarter-Mile Championship for 7th Royal Dublin Fusiliers, St. Patrick's Day, 1915. Now Sergeant.

MacDONALD, CHARLES J.

Born at Brooklyn, New York. Son of the late T. MacDonald. Educated at Ranelagh School. Clerk, Irish Railway Clearing House. Member of Rugby Football Union. Killed in action, August 17, 1915.

McCORMICK, DESMOND N.

Born at Carramore, Co. Mayo. Son of the late S. McCormick. Clerk. Member of Winning Football Team for " Duckett Cup," 1914.

McELLIGOTT, FRANCIS

Born at Listowel, Co. Kerry. Son of G. McElligott, of Listowel. Educated at St. Vincent's College, Castleknock, Co. Dublin. One of the reserves who were left at Mudros and who rejoined Battalion, August 16, 1915. At Suvla, Serbia, Salonika.

WILLIAM T. McCARTHY

ROBERT R. McCULLAGH

WILLIAM McCLELLAND

CHARLES J. MacDONALD

DESMOND N. McCORMICK

FRANCIS McELLIGOTT

McFERRAN, WM. ROBERT

Born at Kingstown, Co. Dublin. Son of Wm. McFerran, Solicitor, of Dublin. Educated at Campbell College, Belfast, and Trinity College, Dublin. Solicitor's Apprentice and Student. Commission, September 14, 1915, in 7th Royal Dublin Fusiliers. At Suvla, Serbia, Salonika.

McMURTRY, ALFRED D.

Born at Belfast. Son of Ch. McMurtry, now of Dublin. Educated at Methodist College, Belfast, and St. Andrew's College, Dublin. Commercial Traveller. Invalided, suffering from frost-bite, December 1915. Now Sergeant.

MacHUTCHISON, WILLIAM F.

Born at Dublin. Son of J. Mac-Hutchison, of Dublin. Educated at St. Andrew's College, Dublin. Official, Hong-Kong and Shanghai Banking Corporation. Transferred from " D " to " A " Company, February 1915. Disembarked at Alexandria, July 24, 1915. Invalided, suffering from enteric, August 12, 1915. Rejoined in October 1915, and is now Quartermaster-Sergeant to 30th Infantry Brigade.

MAHER, PATRICK J.

Born at Ballyfarnon. Son of P. A. Maher. Educated at Castleknock College. Clerk in Hibernian Bank. Gunshot wound in left leg, August 7, 1915. Rejoined Battalion at Salonika, October 1915.

McLACHLAN, EDWARD B.

Born in Dublin. Son of L. McLachlan, of Dublin. Educated at St. Mary's and Sandford Schools. Member of 1st City of Dublin Cadets and of Trojan Football Club. Gun-shot wound in right foot, August 16, 1915. Invalided in October 1915.

MANNING, WILLIAM J.

Born at Kingstown, Co. Dublin. Son of T. J. Manning, of Dublin. Educated at Blackrock College. Civil Servant. One of the reserves left at Mudros who rejoined Battalion, August 16, 1915. Invalided from Serbia with frost-bite and rheumatism, but rejoined Battalion. Killed in France, October 1916.

THE PALS AT SUVLA BAY

WM. ROBERT McFERRAN

ALFRED D. McMURTRY

WILLIAM F. MacHUTCHISON

PATRICK J. MAHER

EDWARD B. McLACHLAN

WILLIAM J. MANNING

MARRABLE, FRANCIS A.

Born at Monkstown, Co. Dublin. Son of A. Marrable, of Cabinteely, Co. Dublin. Educated at Aravon, Bray, and Trinity College, Dublin. Chartered Accountant. Died on homeward-bound transport on August 18, 1915, from wounds received at Suvla.

MEES, ARTHUR J.

Born at Cardiff. Son of W. G. Mees, of Cardiff. Educated at Gladstone Schools, Cardiff. Clerk. One of the reserves left behind at Mudros who rejoined Battalion at Suvla, August 16, 1915.

MATHEWS, WM. F. A.

Son of Marcus B. Mathews, Northern Bank House, Dublin. Educated at St. Andrew's College, Dublin. Member of Wanderers Football Club and Neptune Rowing Club, and rowed stroke for Junior Crew of latter club, 1913-14. Killed in action, September 13, 1915.

MEREDITH, ARTHUR C.

Born at Belfast. Son of the late Major E. T. Meredith, R.E. Mercantile Marine. One of the reserves disembarked at Mudros who rejoined Battalion, August 16, 1915.

MAY, ARTHUR E.

Born at Castlebar, Co. Mayo. Son of T. May, now of Dublin. Educated at Rathmines College, Dublin. Clerk.

MIDDLETON, ALFRED H.

Born at Kingstown, Co. Dublin. Son of T. B. Middleton, of Shankill, Co. Dublin. Educated at Aravon, Co. Wicklow, Lee-on-the-Solent, and Trinity College, Dublin. B.A., Trinity College, Dublin. Gold Medal, Botany and Natural Science. Official, Guinness's Brewery. Gazetted Second Lieutenant Army Service Corps, November 1914. Transferred to 2nd Battalion Munster Fusiliers, 1915.

THE PALS AT SUVLA BAY

FRANCIS A. MARRABLE

ARTHUR J. MEES

WM. F. A. MATHEWS

ARTHUR C. MEREDITH

ARTHUR E. MAY

ALFRED H. MIDDLETON

MILLAR, EDWARD CHAYTOR

Born at Monkstown, Co. Dublin. Son of Fitzadam Millar, of Monkstown. Educated privately and at Trinity College, Dublin. Rowed for Junior Eight, Trinity College, Dublin, for two seasons. Member of Monkstown Football Club and of their 1st xv, 1913 and 1914. Promoted Sergeant, September 1914. Killed whilst exhorting men of another regiment to "stand firm," August 9, 1915. Mentioned in dispatches for "gallant and distinguished conduct in field."

MOORE, WILLIAM E. A.

Born at Dublin. Son of Sir John Moore of same city. Educated at Strangway's School and Trinity College, Dublin. Journalist. Discharged as "medically unfit for Active Service," January 1915.

MITCHELL, JAMES

Born at Knocklong, Co. Limerick. Son of T. Mitchell. Educated at Knocklong and Hospital Schools. Civil Servant, Registry of Deeds, Dublin. Made Lance-Corporal in March 1915, and Corporal in October of same year.

MOORE, WILLIAM MICHAEL

Born at Dublin. Son of E. Moore of that city. Educated at Strangway's School, Dublin, and Campbell College, Belfast. Member of Dublin University Officers' Training Corps. Promoted Lance-Corporal on September 17, 1914, and Corporal at end of same month. Gazetted Second Lieutenant 7th Battalion Royal Irish Fusiliers, October 1914.

MOLONY, WILLINGTON

Born at Dublin. Son of the late D. J. Molony, of Dublin. Educated at Tara College. Chief Clerk, Messrs. Jas. Adam and Son, Dublin. Made Corporal, September 17, 1914, and Sergeant ten days later. Transferred from "D" to "A" Company and made Company Quartermaster-Sergeant, April 1915. Gun-shot wound in thigh, August 7, 1915, and invalided a week later. Gazetted Second Lieutenant Army Service Corps, December 1915. Now Lieutenant, Adjutant, and Second-in-Command of 14th Reserve Park Army Service Corps, France.

MORAN, MICHAEL J.

Born at Dublin. Son of M. Moran. Educated at Castleknock and University Colleges, Dublin. Civil Servant, Land Registry, Dublin. One of the reserves left behind at Mudros who rejoined Battalion at Suvla, August 16, 1915.

EDWARD CHAYTOR MILLAR

WILLIAM E. A. MOORE

JAMES MITCHELL

WILLIAM MICHAEL MOORE

WILLINGTON MOLONY

MICHAEL J. MORAN

MORRISON, H. ST. J. R.

Born at Kingstown, Co. Dublin. Son of J. Morrison, now of Sandycove, Co. Dublin. Educated at Wesley College, Mountjoy School, and Trinity College, Dublin. Invalided, suffering from dysentery, August 26, 1915. Gazetted Second Lieutenant 7th Royal Dublin Fusiliers, December 1915.

MURRAY, WILLIAM C.

Born at Bannon, Co. Wexford. Son of the late Rev. W. D. Murray. Educated privately and at Rosse College, Dublin. Clerk, Bank of Ireland, Dublin. Killed in action, August 16, 1915.

MOSS, ARNOLD W.

Born at Stillorgan, Co. Dublin. Son of H. W. Moss. Educated at Strangway's School and Trinity College, Dublin. Was a Member of Dublin University Officers' Training Corps. Made Lance-Corporal, August 14, 1915. Missing since bayonet charge on August 16, 1915. Recommended for D.C.M. for assisting wounded comrades under fire, August 9, 1915. Brother of Second-Lieutenant G. L. Moss (Military Cross).

MURPHY, RICHARD V.

Born near Borris, Co. Carlow. Son of the late W. A. Murphy, of Gowram, Co. Kilkenny. Educated at Kilkenny College, Collegiate School, Portarlington, and Mountjoy School, Dublin. Civil Servant, Registry of Titles, Dublin. Member of Wanderers Football Club. Promoted Lance-Corporal, September 1915.

MURRAY, ALFRED H.

Born at Ballymena, Co. Antrim. Son of Mrs. Murray, 33 Waterloo Road, Dublin. Educated at Ballymena Academy and at Portsmouth Grammar School. Inspector in Scottish Widows' Fund Society. Promoted Sergeant, August 13, 1915. Commissioned, September 14, 1915, to 7th Royal Dublin Fusiliers. At Suvla. Serbia, Salonika.

MYLES, FINLAY

Born at Sandymount, Dublin. Son of J. Myles, of Dublin. Civil Servant. Promoted Sergeant in September 1914, and Company Quartermaster-Sergeant in February 1915. Slightly wounded in retreat from Serbia, but has since rejoined the Battalion at Salonika.

THE PALS AT SUVLA BAY

H. ST. J. R. MORRISON

WILLIAM C. MURRAY

ARNOLD W. MOSS

RICHARD V. MURPHY

ALFRED H. MURRAY

FINLAY MYLES

NAGLE, WILLIAM JOS.

Born in Dublin. Son of J. Nagle, of Dublin. Educated at Central Model Schools, Dublin. Farmer. Made Lance-Corporal, August 14, 1915.

O'GRADY, WILLIAM M.

Born at Dublin. Son of Bernard O'Grady, of Dublin. Educated at Wesley College. Solicitor. Gazetted Second Lieutenant 14th Manchester Regiment, November 1914. Attached to 8th Manchester Regiment in Egypt. Transferred to 7th Royal Munster Fusiliers at Salonika.

NOLAN, EDWARD W.

Born at Tullow, Co. Carlow. Son of late Dr. J. Nolan, of Tullow. Educated at Castleknock College. Gentleman Farmer. One of the reserves left at Mudros who rejoined Battalion, August 16, 1915.

OLDHAM, ELDON A. S.

Born at Dalkey, Co. Dublin. Son of W. M. Oldham, now of Dublin. Educated at Morgan's School, Castleknock. Chemist's Assistant. Invalided, suffering from debility, November 1915. Rejoined Battalion, February 1916. Again invalided with rheumatic fever, April 1916.

NORMAN, CONNOLLY G.

Born at Fahan, Co. Donegal. Son of Robt. Norman, now of Bedford. Educated at Bedford Grammar School. Official, Guinness's Brewery. Made Lance-Corporal, August 16, 1915. Invalided, suffering from enteric and jaundice, September 1915. Now training for Commission in Cadet Corps, Curragh.

O'LOUGHLIN, MICHAEL M.

Born at Dublin. Son of M. O'Loughlin. Educated at St. Joseph's College, Clondalkin. Civil Servant. Member of Commercial Rowing Club and Clonliffe Harriers. Won Hovan Cup, 1910. Second in Doran Shield, 1911. Was attached to Army Service Corps in Boer War. One of the reserves left at Mudros who rejoined Battalion, August 16, 1915.

THE PALS AT SUVLA BAY

WILLIAM JOS. NAGLE

WILLIAM M. O'GRADY

EDWARD W. NOLAN

ELDON A. S. OLDHAM

CONNOLLY G. NORMAN

MICHAEL M. O'LOUGHLIN

O'NEILL, CHARLES

Born at Dollymount, Co. Dublin. Son of H. G. O'Neill, of Dublin. Educated at Clontarf and privately. Clerk, Bank of Ireland. Gun-shot wound in right thigh and dysentery, August 22, 1915. Invalided two days later. One of the reserves landed at Mudros who rejoined Battalion, August 16, 1915. Now Corporal, attached to 10th Battalion Royal Dublin Fusiliers.

PARRY, STANLEY KAYE

Born at Kingstown, Co. Dublin. Son of W. Kaye Parry. Educated at Trent College, Derbyshire, and Trinity College, Dublin. B.A. (Trinity College, Dublin). Chartered Accountant. Made Lance-Corporal, January 1915, and Corporal a week later; Lance-Sergeant, August 1915. Gazetted Second Lieutenant 7th Royal Dublin Fusiliers, September 1915.

O'SULLIVAN, GARTH R.

Born at Dublin. Son of the late Dr. J. A. O'Sullivan, of Ballsbridge, Co. Dublin. Educated at St. Vincent's College, Castleknock. Apprentice, Mercantile Marine (Lord Line). Invalided, suffering from dysentery, August 1915. Gazetted Second Lieutenant 6th Royal Irish Rifles, December 1915.

PAUL, CHARLES A.

Born at Dublin. Son of C. J. Paul, of Dublin. Educated at Howth Road and Wesley College, Dublin. Insurance Clerk. Made Lance-Corporal, August 1915. Invalided, suffering from dysentery, August 24, 1915. Gazetted Second Lieutenant 6th Royal Dublin Fusiliers, December 1915. Now serving at Salonika.

PARKES, FITZWILLIAM C. O'G.

Born at Amritsar, Punjab, India. Son of B. Parkes, now of Castletown, Isle of Man. Educated at King William's College, Isle of Man, and Trinity College, Dublin. Gun-shot wound in left shoulder, August 9, 1915. Now with Battalion at Salonika.

PAUL, WALTER C.

Born at Dublin. Brother of C. A. Paul. Educated at Howth Road and Wesley College, Dublin. Captain of Clontarf Rugby Football Schoolboy Team for several seasons. Killed in action, Suvla Landing, August 7, 1915.

CHARLES O'NEILL

STANLEY KAYE PARRY

GARTH R. O'SULLIVAN

CHARLES A. PAUL

FITZWILLIAM C. O'G. PARKES

WALTER C. PAUL

PIGOTT, ANDREW C.

Born in Belfast. Son of D. Pigott. Educated at St. Andrew's College, Dublin. Transferred to 3rd Battalion Royal Dublin Fusiliers, July 1915.

POLLOCK, HUGO C.

Born at Dublin. Son of Hugh Pollock. Educated at St. Andrew's College, Dublin. Assistant Manager of tea estates in Sumatra ; came home to join Army. Member of Wanderers Football Club. Missing since August 16, 1915.

PERRY, JOHN J.

Born at Dublin. Son of Geo. Perry, of Dublin. Educated at St. George's College, Weybridge. Director, G. Perry and Co., Ltd., Dublin. Made Lance-Corporal, January 1915 ; Corporal, August 1915.

POOLE, HENRY

Born at Gorey, Co. Wexford. Son of R. Poole, of Gorey. Educated at The Taire School, Wexford. Accountant, Provincial Bank, Cork. One of the Transport who embarked with Sir Stanley Cochrane, October 14, and joined Battalion at Salonika, October 26, 1915.

PHILLIPS, FRANK N.

Born at Kinsale, Co. Cork. Son of the late M. Phillips, of Enniscorthy. Member of Waterford Boat Club, and played Football for several clubs in Waterford. Invalided, suffering from gun-shot wounds, August 7, 1915, and rejoined Battalion, October 1915. Again invalided, suffering from dysentery, December 1915, but has since rejoined Battalion at Salonika.

POULTER, EDGAR A.

Born in London. Son of H. C. Poulter, now of Dundrum, Co. Dublin. Educated at St. Andrew's College, Dublin. Clerk, North British and Mercantile Insurance Company. Made Lance-Corporal, March 1915 ; Corporal, October 1915. Invalided from Salonika, suffering from typhoid, March 1916.

THE PALS AT SUVLA BAY

ANDREW C. PIGOTT

HUGO C. POLLOCK

JOHN J. PERRY

HENRY POOLE

FRANK N. PHILLIPS

EDGAR A. POULTER

225

POULTER, HENRY CHAPMAN

Born in London. Brother of E. A. Poulter. Educated at St. Andrew's College, Dublin. Clerk, Atlas Insurance Company. Invalided, suffering from enteric, October 26, 1915. Gazetted Second Lieutenant 7th Royal Dublin Fusiliers, February 1916.

PROSSER, JOHN H.

Born at Cardiff. Son of W. Prosser, of Cardiff. Educated at Cardiff Intermediate School. Commercial Traveller. Disembarked, Alexandria, July 24, 1915. Invalided, suffering from rheumatism, October 1915, but rejoined Battalion a month later.

POULTON, GEORGE V.

Born at Dublin. Son of J. V. Poulton. Educated at St. Andrew's College. Commercial Traveller. Invalided, suffering from enteric, August 30, 1916, and has not yet sufficiently recovered to rejoin.

RAINFORD, GEORGE H.

Born at Kirkby Bedon, Norfolk. Son of W. A. Rainford. Educated at Poringland and Rushford Schools, Norfolk. Embarked with transport, October 14, 1915, and joined Battalion at Salonika, October 26, 1915.

PRICE, JOHN L.

Born at Clonmel, Co. Tipperary. Son of H. Price, of Rathkeale, Co. Limerick. Educated at Christian Brothers Schools, Tipperary; St. Brendan's, Killarney, and Hughes's Academy Belfast. Secondary Teacher. Shrapnel wound right side, August 7, 1915. Rejoined, October 1915.

REID, ROBERT F.

Born at Tralee, Co. Kerry. Son of Lewis Reid, now of Dublin. Educated at Tralee. Clerk.

THE PALS AT SUVLA BAY

HENRY CHAPMAN POULTER

JOHN H. PROSSER

GEORGE V. POULTON

GEORGE H RAINFORD

JOHN L. PRICE

ROBERT F. REID

REID, WILLIAM STANLEY

Born at Dublin. Son of Henry Reid. Educated at Glasnevin, Dublin. Invalided, April 12, 1916.

ROBERTS, J. W.

Born at Lough Rynn, Co. Leitrim. Son of the late Richard Croker Roberts. Educated at Masonic School, Dublin. Clerk in G.S.W. Railway (Ireland). Commission, September 14, 1915, 5th Royal Inniskilling Fusiliers. Suvla, etc.

RICHARDSON, M. P. V.

Born at Dundrum, Co. Dublin. Son of J. Richardson, of Dundrum. Educated at St. Mary's College, Rathmines, Dublin. Killed in action, September 4, 1915.

ROBERTSON, WILLIAM H.

Born at Dublin. Son of W. Robertson, of Dublin. Educated at St. Patrick's School, Dublin. One of the reserves left at Mudros who rejoined Battalion, August 16, 1915. Made Lance-Corporal, September 20, 1915. Invalided, suffering from rheumatism, December 1915.

ROBERTS, HAROLD

Born at Barby. Son of A. Roberts, of Barby (near Rugby). Invalided, suffering from broncho-pneumonia, November 17, 1915.

RONALDSON, GEORGE E.

Born at Leixlip, Co. Kildare. Son of W. R. Ronaldson, of Leixlip. Educated at St. Andrew's College, Dublin. Missing since August 16, 1915.

WILLIAM STANLEY REID

J. W. ROBERTS

M. P. V. RICHARDSON

WILLIAM H. ROBERTSON

HAROLD ROBERTS

GEORGE E. RONALDSON

RUSSELL, NORMAN

Born at Dublin. Son of J. Russell, of Dublin. Educated at The Castle School, Sandymount, Co. Dublin. Book-keeper. Made Corporal, September 17, 1914, and Sergeant a fortnight later. Gazetted Second Lieutenant Army Service Corps, October 1914. Wounded at Gallipoli in September 1915, and invalided home. Now in England with Army Service Corps.

SCOTT, ALEXANDER

Born at Gorey, Co. Wexford. Son of J. A. Scott. Educated at King's Hospital, Dublin. First-class Clerk, Guinness's Brewery. Transferred from " D " to " B " Company (Machine-Gun Section), April 1915.

SARGAISON, WM. H.

Born at Longford. Son of W. Sargaison. Educated at Mountjoy School, Dublin, and St. George's School, London. Clerk, Irish Lights Office, Dublin. Made Lance-Corporal, August 7, 1915, and Corporal a week later. Gazetted Second Lieutenant 5th Battalion Connaught Rangers, September 1916. Killed by a high-explosive shell in retreat from Serbia, December 6, 1915.

SEDDON, JAMES

Born at Wigan, Lancashire. Son of J. Seddon. Educated at Wigan, Haydock, and St. Helens. Transferred from " D " to " A " Company, February 1915. Made Corporal, February 24, Lance-Sergeant, June 23, and Sergeant, August 16, 1915. Gun-shot wound in chest and pleurisy, August 20, 1915. Invalided four days later.

SCALES, RICHARD D.

Born in Dublin. Son of R. Scales, of Dublin. Educated at Wesley College, Dublin. Civil Servant. Member of Olney Hockey and Lawn Tennis Clubs. Gun-shot wound right shoulder, August 12, 1915. Rejoined at Alexandria six weeks later, but was invalided home, suffering from dysentery, in October 1915. Now attached to 10th Royal Dublin Fusiliers.

SELFE, EDWIN A. W.

Born at Dublin. Son of the late E. S. Selfe, of Dublin. Educated at St. Patrick's Cathedral Grammar School, Dublin. Member of Mixed Vocal Quartet which won Gold Medal, Feis, 1914. Clerk, D. and S.E. Railway. Enteric fever, February 1916. Now invalided home.

NORMAN RUSSELL

ALEXANDER SCOTT

WM. H. SARGAISON

JAMES SEDDON

RICHARD D. SCALES

EDWIN A. W. SELFE

SHANAGHER, DENIS P.

Born in Belfast. Son of D. Shanagher. Educated at St. Paul's and Hughes's Academy, Belfast, and King's College, London. Civil Servant. Transferred from " D " to " B " Company (Machine-Gun Section), April 1915.

SHERWOOD, THOMAS B.

Born at Eccles, Lancashire. Son of T. B. Sherwood. Educated at Eccles and Manchester Grammar Schools. Official, Commercial Union Insurance Company, Dublin. One of the reserves left at Mudros who rejoined Battalion, August 16, 1915. Transferred from " D " to " B " Company (Machine-Gun Section), September 14, 1915, and made Lance-Corporal on same date.

SHAW, J. H. DE B.

Born at Cloncallow, Co. Longford. Son of the late John Shaw. Educated at Corrig School, Kingstown, and Trinity College, Dublin. Barrister.

STEPHEN, WILLIAM CAREY

Born at Dublin. Son of R. Stephen, of Dublin. Educated at Howth Road and Sandymount Academical Institute, Dublin. Accountant.

SHEIL, CHARLES

Born at Dublin. Son of R. H. Sheil, of Dublin. Educated at Clongowes Wood School and Royal College of Science, Dublin. Member of Brewhouse Staff, Guinness's Brewery. Made Lance-Corporal, January 17, 1915. Gun-shot wound right thigh, August 16, 1915. Rejoined Battalion in October 1915.

STRAHAN, ANDREW H.

Born in Dublin. Son of A. Strahan, of Clontarf, Dublin. Educated at Mountjoy School, Dublin. Articled Clerk to Chartered Accountant. Gunshot wound in back, August 28, 1915. Invalided, September 1915. Was attached to 10th Royal Dublin Fusiliers, and is now in Cadet Corps, Curragh. Present rank, Sergeant.

DENIS P. SHANAGHER

THOMAS B. SHERWOOD

J. H. DE B. SHAW

WILLIAM CAREY STEPHEN

CHARLES SHEIL

ANDREW H. STRAHAN

SWAN, RICHARD S.

Born in Dublin. Son of T. E. Swan. Educated at High School, Dublin. Clerk, Bank of Ireland, Dublin. Member of Lansdowne 1st Rugby Football Team, Mount Temple Tennis Club, Rathfarnham Golf Club, and Castlecomer Cricket Club. Died of typhoid fever, Salonika, August 9, 1916.

THOMPSON, FREDERICK R.

Born in Dublin. Son of F. J. Thompson. Educated at Corrig School, Kingstown, and Royal School, Dungannon. One of the reserves left at Mudros who rejoined Battalion, August 16, 1915.

SYMES, THOMAS A.

Born at Hill View, Co. Wexford. Son of S. J. Symes. Educated privately. Clerk, Bank of Ireland. Disembarked at Mudros, July 30 ; developed dysentery in August, of which he died in 2nd Australian Hospital, Mudros, on August 18, 1915.

THORNTON, HENRY

Born in Dublin. Son of Ernest Charles Thornton of same place. Educated at Diocesan School, Dublin. Decorative Artist. Holder of Irish Middleweight Championship for Wrestling. Lance-Corporal, December 12, 1914 ; Sergeant, February 24, 1915. Transferred from " D " to " A " Company, February 27, 1915. Suvla. Wounded, Kizlar Dagh, August 16, 1915.

TAYLOR, ARTHUR McC.

Born in Dublin. Son of A. Taylor. Educated at St. Andrew's College, Dublin. One of the reserves left at Mudros who rejoined Battalion, August 16, 1915. Transferred to Machine-Gun Section, August 1915.

TIERNEY, HERBERT S.

Born in Dublin. Son of C. Tierney. Educated at Prior Park, Bath ; Belvidere College, Dublin, and Royal University, Ireland. B.A. (Royal University, Ireland). Barrister. Gazetted Second Lieutenant 8th Battalion Cheshire Regiment, November 1914. With force which tried to relieve General Townshend in Kut-el-Amara. Missing since April 9, 1916.

THE PALS AT SUVLA BAY

RICHARD S. SWAN

FREDERICK R. THOMPSON

THOMAS A. SYMES

HENRY THORNTON

ARTHUR McC. TAYLOR

HERBERT S. TIERNEY

TITTLE, J. H. VOS

Born at Straffan, Co. Kildare. Son of David R. Tittle, now of Foxrock, Co. Dublin. Educated at Royal School, Armagh. Discharged as " medically unfit," December 1915.

VALENTINE, ROBERT L.

Born at Portora, Enniskillen. Son of W. J. Valentine. Educated at High School and College of Science, Dublin. Associate, Royal College of Science (Ireland). Junior Geologist, Irish Geological Survey. Gazetted Second Lieutenant 8th Royal Dublin Fusiliers, October 1914. Promoted Lieutenant. Invented contrivance for quick-filling of Lewis ·303 machine-gun, which was accepted by War Office. Killed in action at Loos, April 30, 1916.

TOBIN, RICHARD PATRICK

Son of Lieutenant-Colonel R. F. Tobin, Royal Army Medical Corps, Dublin. Educated at St. Stephen's Green School, Dublin, and Trinity College, Dublin. Student. Gazetted 7th Royal Dublin Fusiliers, August 1914; Captaincy, July 1915. Killed at Kiretch Tepe Sirt, Suvla Bay, August 16, 1915, aged twenty-one years. Mentioned in dispatches for " distinguished gallantry in the field."

WALKEY, FRANCIS A.

Born at Dublin. Son of C. H. Walkey, of Dublin. Educated at Wesley College, Dublin, and Truro College, Cornwall. Civil Servant. Invalided to Malta, suffering from dysentery, September 1915, and afterwards sent to Alexandria.

TRIMBLE, AILWYN E. C.

Born at Enniskillen. Son of W. Trimble, of Enniskillen. Educated at Royal School, Portora. Divinity Student, Magee College, Londonderry. Gazetted Second Lieutenant 7th Royal Inniskilling Fusiliers, September 29, 1914. Twice mentioned in dispatches.

WATTS, J. ATTWOOD

Born at Dublin. Son of W. J. Watts, of Drumcondra, Dublin. Educated at Mountjoy School, Dublin. On Staff of Department of Agriculture (Ireland). Made Lance-Corporal, December 1914; Corporal, January 1915; and Sergeant, February 1915. Transferred from " D " to " A " Company, February 1915. Gun-shot wound in mouth, August 16, 1915. Now gazetted Second Lieutenant South Irish Horse.

THE PALS AT SUVLA BAY

J. H. VOS TITTLE

ROBERT L. VALENTINE

RICHARD PATRICK TOBIN

FRANCIS A. WALKEY

AILWYN E. C. TRIMBLE

J. ATTWOOD WATTS

WEATHERILL, EDWARD T.

Born at Dublin. Son of Captain J. Weatherill. Educated at St. Andrew's College, Dublin ; Fettes College, Edinburgh ; and Armstrong College, Newcastle-on-Tyne. Partner in firm of J. Weatherill and Sons, Dublin. Made Sergeant Machine-Gun Section, December 1914. Transferred from " D " to " B " Company, December 1914. Gazetted Second Lieutenant 7th Royal Dublin Fusiliers, March 1915. Member of Monkstown and Lansdowne Road Football Club. Killed in action, August 16, 1915. Reported to have rescued five wounded.

WINTER, JOS. ALEX.

Born in Dublin. Son of J. P. Winter, of Dublin. Educated at Mountjoy School, Dublin. Clerk, Sun Insurance Company, Dublin. Gun-shot wound left cheek and shoulder, August 16, 1915. Invalided, September 15, 1915. Now Sergeant on Permanent Staff, Irish Command Depot, Tipperary.

WHITTAKER, JOHN H. E.

Born at Dublin. Son of Deputy-Surgeon-General J. H. Whittaker, Royal Army Medical Corps. Educated at Cheltenham College and Trinity College, Dublin. Gazetted Second Lieutenant 8th Inniskilling Fusiliers, September 1914. Now Lieutenant.

WOOD, NORMAN

Born at Galway. Son of George Wood, of Dublin. Educated at St. Andrew's College, Dublin, and Royal School, Portora. On No. 1 Staff, Guinness's Brewery, Dublin. Member of Wanderers Football and Dublin Swimming Clubs. Made Lance-Corporal, January 1915 ; Sergeant, February 1915. Transferred from " D " to " A " Company, February 1915. Gun-shot wound and fracture left thigh, August 7, 1915. Invalided, August 17, 1915.

WHITTY, THOMAS A.

Born at Waterford. Son of the late Dr. P. J. Whitty, of Blackrock, Co. Dublin. Educated at Castleknock College, Co. Dublin. Civil Servant. Made Lance-Corporal, January 1915. Missing since August 16, 1915.

WOODMAN, CLIFFORD

Born at Dublin. Son of G. Woodman, of Dublin. Educated at Wesley College, Dublin.

EDWARD T. WEATHERILL

JOS. ALEX. WINTER

JOHN H. E. WHITTAKER

NORMAN WOOD

THOMAS A. WHITTY

CLIFFORD WOODMAN

WOODMAN, WILLIAM J. A.

Born in Dublin. Brother of C. Woodman. Educated at Mountjoy School, Dublin. Clerk in Cook's Tourist Agency. Made Lance-Corporal, March 1915, and Corporal, August 1915. Gunshot wounds in right shoulder and left elbow, August 21, 1915, but rejoined next day. Invalided to Cairo, suffering from septic wounds, December 1915.

WILLIAM J. A. WOODMAN

WOODS, WILLIAM W.

Born at Listowel, Co. Kerry. Son of W. Woods. Educated at Rathmines College, Dublin. Insurance Clerk. One of the reserves landed at Mudros who rejoined Battalion, August 16, 1915. Invalided to Malta, suffering from rheumatic fever, May 1916.

WILLIAM W. WOODS

YOUNG, WM. JOHN

Born in Dublin. Fourth son of Dr. B. P. Young, Royal Army Medical Corps. Educated at High School, Dublin. Played for Clontarf and Lansdowne Football Clubs. Enlisted September 1914. Transferred to Machine-Gun Section. Served at Suvla and Salonika. Promoted Corporal, February 1916.

WM. JOHN YOUNG

BIOGRAPHICAL NOTES OF THOSE OF WHOM NO PHOTOGRAPHS WERE AVAILABLE

BLACK, F. J.
Private. Wounded, Suvla, August 7, 1915.

BRABAZON, A.
Commission, September 22, 1914.

BRADBURNE, EDWARD STEPHEN
Born at Dublin. Son of Stephen M. Bradburne, of Donnybrook, Dublin. Educated at Dublin. Clerk. Disembarked, Alexandria, July 21, 1915, to act as Company Storeman at that place.

BRADY, A.
Private. Wounded, Suvla, August 7, 1915.

BRADY, JOSEPH
Born at Belfast. Professional Billiard Player. Made Lance-Corporal, August 14, 1915. Stretcher-bearer. Enteric, August 20, 1915; invalided four days later. Now Corporal, attached to 10th Royal Dublin Fusiliers.

BROWN, N. W.
Lance-Corporal. Shrapnel wound, August 7, 1915. Rejoined, October 2, 1915, as interpreter in France.

CARRIG, T. B.

CASSIDY, PATRICK J.
Born in Dublin. Son of Daniel Cassidy. Civil Servant, General Valuation Office. Corporal. Transferred from " D " to " A," September 28, 1914. Promoted Corporal, June 14, 1915. Wounded, Suvla, August 7, 1915. Wounded in both legs in Serbia. Subsequently promoted to rank of Warrant Officer.

CLARKE, J. R. R.
Transferred " D " to " B," December 1, 1914 (Machine-Gun). Lance-Corporal, March 1, 1915; Sergeant, March 9, 1915. Commission, 7th Royal Dublin Fusiliers, September 14, 1915.

CLIFFORD, FRANK D'ARCY
Born at Dublin. Son of Major L. J. Clifford. Educated at Downs School and privately. Transferred to 5th Royal Dublin Fusiliers, March 15, 1915.

COFFEY, W.
Wounded, Kizlar Dagh, August 16, 1915.

CONNOLLY, RICHARD W.
Born at Dublin. Son of Frederick Connolly, of Drumcondra, Dublin. Educated at Christian Brothers School, Dublin. Commercial Traveller. Gunshot wound, from which he lost sight of one eye, August 16, 1915, and was invalided, September 15, 1915. Was made Lance-Corporal (unpaid), June 5, 1915, and Acting Lance-Corporal, August 9, 1915.

THE PALS AT SUVLA BAY

CREAGH, ROBERT J.

Born at Portsmouth. Son of late Lieutenant L. S. Creagh, R.N. Educated at Grammar School, Newcastle-on-Tyne, and Mathematical School, Rochester. Agent. One of the reserves landed at Mudros who rejoined Battalion, August 16, 1915. Invalided home suffering from enteric, November 1915.

CROSS, GEORGE HERBERT

Born at Edinburgh. Son of the late Wm. H. Cross. Educated at Cork Grammar School and High School, Dublin. He was gazetted to the Army Service Corps, November 1914, and now holds the rank of Captain.

CURTIS, D.

Sergeant, January 25, 1915; Acting Quartermaster-Sergeant to 30th Infantry Brigade, March 1, 1915.

DALE, T. S.

Lance-Corporal, December 12, 1914; Corporal, April 21, 1915; Sergeant, August 7, 1915.

DALTON, ALFRED

Born at Cork. Son of A. Dalton, of Cork. Educated at Model School and Skerry's College, Cork. Clerk, G. S. and W. Railway. Invalided, suffering from septic blisters, August 14, 1915, but rejoined Battalion eight days later. Gazetted Second Lieutenant 1st Battalion Royal Dublin Fusiliers, August 14, 1915, and now serving with this Battalion in France.

DIXON, THOMAS VICTOR

Born at Sligo. Son of Joseph H. Dixon, now of Dublin. Educated at Sligo and Preston School, Abbeyleix. Commercial Clerk. Prior to the war was a Lance-Corporal in the 1st City of Dublin Cadet Corps. He was one of the Transport Section.

DIXON, D. J.

Signaller.

DOLAN, GEORGE

Born at Boynagh, Co. Meath. Son of James Dolan. Educated at O'Brien Institute, Dublin. Clerk in Four Courts, Dublin.

DORAN, F. H.

Lance-Corporal, September 7, 1914; Commission, 7th Royal Dublin Fusiliers, September 22, 1914; Lieutenant, October 3, 1915.

DOOLEY, CHARLES HENRY

Born at Gibraltar. Son of the late Lieutenant-Colonel G. F. Dooley. Insurance Agent. Returned from Canada and joined " D " Company. Invalided, suffering from bronchitis, November 1915, but now rejoined Battalion and at Salonika.

EASTWOOD, J. W.

Invalided, September 10, 1915.

GLYNN, E.

Private.

GORDON, J.

Private. With Transport.

GUILFOYLE, E.

Private. Wounded, August 7, 1915, Suvla.

HANNA, JOHN E.

Born at Belfast. Son of J. Hanna, of Belfast. Civil Servant. Educated at Model School and Academical Institution, Belfast.

HAYDEN, BERNARD H. F. E.

Born in London. Son of Captain H. H. Hayden. Educated at Belvidere College, Dublin. Civil Servant. Prior to the war was Second Lieutenant in Dublin Schools Cadet Corps. Owing to this experience was made Sergeant the day after his enlistment. Gazetted Second Lieutenant 6th Royal Welsh Fusiliers, March 1915. Present with his Battalion at Suvla landing and subsequent operations.

242

THE PALS AT SUVLA BAY

HAZLITT, JAMES B.
Born at Fethard, Co. Tipperary. Son of J. Hazlitt, now of Dublin. Educated at Educational Institution, Dundalk, and King's Hospital, Dublin. Student, Ross College, Stephen's Green, Dublin.

HICKEY, C.
Private. Invalided, October 29, 1915.

HOUSTON, THOMAS
Born at Irvine, N.B. Son of T. Houston, now of Belfast. Educated at Belfast. Clerk in Ulster Bank. Transferred from "D" Company to Machine-Gun Section "B" Company, December 1914.

HUGHES, J. W.
Commission, October 5, 1915.

HUNTER, A. P.
Wounded (accidentally), August 31, 1915. Commissioned, September 14, 1915, to 5th Royal Irish Regiment (Pioneers).

JAMESON, JOHN F.
Born at Dublin. Son of J. G. Jameson, now of Malahide, Co. Dublin. Educated at St. Leonards and Frome. Gazetted Second Lieutenant 8th Battalion Royal Dublin Fusiliers, September 1914. Afterwards transferred to Army Service Corps.

JOHN, P. R.
Private. Wounded, Kizlar Dagh, August 15, 1915.

JOHN, W. R.
Private. Enteric, August 30, 1915.

KING, G. A.
Commission, November 26, 1914.

LEAHY, D. O'M.
Commission, February 19, 1915.

LYLE, T.
Commission, September 30, 1914.

MacNIE, G. F.
Born in Dublin. Elder son of Geo. MacNie, of Dublin. Educated at St. Andrew's College, Dublin. Farmer in Argentine. Enlisted, September 16, 1914. Commission, 7th Royal Dublin Fusiliers, November 6, 1914. Transferred 5th Connaught Rangers. Served with them in Serbia and France. Killed in France, September 5, 1916.

MILLER, EDWARD G.
Born in Montgomeryshire. Son of H. Miller, now of Hampstead, London. Educated at King's College School, Chester. Buyer for Messrs. Forrest and Co., Dublin. Gun-shot wound in face, August 5, 1915, but rejoined three days later.

MOUNT, W. J.
Of Belturbet, Co. Cavan. Enlisted, August 21, 1914. Promoted Lance-Corporal, June 5, 1915. Commissioned, September 14, 1915, to 1st Royal Dublin Fusiliers. Invalided, and subsequently transferred to 10th Royal Dublin Fusiliers. Reported "missing" in France, October 1916.

MOYNAGH, STEPHEN HUGH
Son of M. C. Moynagh, Dundalk. Educated at Christian Brothers Schools and St. Mary's College, Dundalk, Solicitor. Discharged from 7th Royal Dublin Fusiliers, being medically unfit, December 1914. Obtained Commission (Second Lieutenant unattached) and served as Recruiting Officer in Newry from June to December 1915, when he resigned.

MURRAY, THOMAS R.
Born at Tralee, Co. Kerry. Son of W. H. Murray. Educated at Christian Brothers Schools, Dublin. Civil Servant, Irish Land Commission. Gun-shot wound in left heel, August 7, 1915. Rejoined, October 1915.

O'GORMAN, M.
Lance-Corporal, February 25, 1915. Transferred from "D" to "A," February 27, 1915. Sergeant, August 7, 1915. Wounded, Suvla, August 21, 1915. Suvla, Salonika.

THE PALS AT SUVLA BAY

PENNEFATHER, RICHARD K.

Born at Thurles, Co. Tipperary. Son of T. B. Pennefather. Educated at Clonmel Grammar School. In Mercantile Marine Service. Invalided, suffering from rheumatism, October 1915. Now attached to 10th Royal Dublin Fusiliers.

PHILIPPE, DOUGLAS G.

Born at Bray, Co. Wicklow. Son of J. Philippe, of Dublin. Educated at St. Andrew's College, Dublin. Clerk.

REDDY, THOMAS F.

Born at Dublin. Educated at St. Mary's College, Rathmines, Dublin. Civil Servant. Made Lance-Corporal, September 1915. Accidental bomb wound in right hand, November 1915.

REID, ALEXANDER W. D.

Born at Brighton. Son of A. Reid. Educated at Strangway's School and Trinity College, Dublin. B.A. (Trinity College, Dublin). Gazetted Second Lieutenant 13th Durham Light Infantry, October 1914. Promoted Captain, 1915; Adjutant 23rd Infantry Base Depot, France, February 1916.

ROBB, G. F.

Private. Killed, Kizlar Dagh, August 16, 1915.

ROSS, F. A.

Of Dublin. Lance-Corporal, January 1, 1915; Corporal, August 16, 1915; Sergeant, September 14, 1915.

SUTCLIFFE, R. S.

Lance-Corporal, September 28, 1914; Corporal, December 12, 1914; Sergeant, January 7, 1915. Wounded, Suvla, August 10, 1915. Commission, 7th Royal Dublin Fusiliers.

SYNNOTT, E. F.

Private. Wounded, Kizlar Dagh, August 16, 1915.

TRAVERS, M. T. L.

Commission, December 22, 1914.

VERDON, E. H.

Lance-Corporal, August 16, 1915. Commission, September 14, 1915, 5th Royal Irish Fusiliers.

WATTS, SYDNEY C.

Born at Brighton. Son of F. E. Watts, of Brighton. Educated at Christ Church and Science Schools, Brighton. Made Lance-Corporal, June 1915. Shrapnel wound in left shoulder, August 8; invalided, September 15, 1915.

WHITEHEAD, W.

Lance-Corporal. Left with transport, July 9, 1915. Discharged.

WILKIN, A. E.

Private. Killed, Kizlar Dagh, August 16, 1915. Mentioned in dispatches for distinguished gallantry in action.

PRINTED AT THE COMPLETE PRESS
WEST NORWOOD
LONDON